In this the love of God was manifested toward us,

that God has sent His only begotten Son into the world,

that we might live through Him.

~ 1 John 4:9 ~

For He made Him who knew no sin

to be sin for us,

that we might become the righteousness of God in Him.

~ 2 Corinthians 5:21~

Tim,

Until Christ is formed in us.
(Galatians 4:19)-

Bill Day

Becoming the Likeness of Jesus

and

becoming yourself at the same time

Bill Day

Pyramid Publishers
1314 Grandview Circle
Buffalo, Minnesota 55313
763.486.2867
patrickday@pyramidpublishers.com

ISBN – 978-0-9982014-4-3 (digital)
ISBN – 978-0-9982014-3-6 (print)

Cover Painting "Two Hearts Beat As One" Copyright © by Stephen Anderson
Prints available at: stephen-anderson.pixels.com
Cover Design by Stan Elder
Interior Design and Layout by
Just Ink Digital Design

Printed in the United States of America

To Andrew Murray (1828-1917)
a fellow journeyman who labored in a vineyard for years
so that Jesus' vine and branches image could come alive in his soul.
Then he wrote *Abide in Christ* and *The True Vine*, two works
which God has used mightily in preparing my heart
for His transformation. Andrew Murray was a prolific writer,
and many of his works illumine the secret of the Vine.
I dedicate this book to him in remembrance and gratitude.

Preface

Becoming the Likeness of Jesus is expository writing anchored in autobiography. The format is *story*. This book is not a personal history of my life, though it is a story told within the context of my life. And my life is only somewhat unusual: a Catholic seminarian who becomes an atheist, a humanistic psychologist, a New Age devotee, and finally a believer in Jesus.

However, there is a story within my struggles and failures, my dead ends and shattered dreams, my search for peace and happiness. It is the story of *everyman,* the human story. We all are fellow travelers on this planet, sometimes unsure of why we are here at all. Anyone's story may overlap or touch upon commonalities that we all share.

A golden thread runs through the human story, and this thread is the story of Jesus. His Incarnation began with birth in a stable, an event that happened so He could be born into our hearts. *Becoming the Likeness of Jesus* is the story of how the Incarnation becomes a transformation rippling out from Jesus' death and resurrection . . . flowing into us today as we acknowledge our old selves to be dead and replaced by His resurrected life. In Him we are new creations.

From this perspective, Jesus' life is intertwined with a believer's life in ways that illumine God's intentions. The core conclusion I have come to is that our transformed life in Jesus is what each of us has been created to be. Hence the subtitle, *and becoming yourself at the same time.*

I have refrained from making *general* statements ("as we know"), or *declarative* statements ("this is the way it is"), or *authoritative* statements ("you should see it this way"). Sometimes I speak passionately, out of strength of conviction, and sometimes I give interpretations and judgments of texts and events. Whatever the case, I acknowledge all statements herein as my own, except where noted otherwise.

~ Bill Day

CHAPTER CONTENTS

PART I
Long Day's Journey Through Night and into the Light

PART II
The Dynamics of Transformation

PART III
The Intention of Transformation

Introduction

A wondrous treasure lies buried in the depths of the Gospel. Many know of this treasure but do not realize that it is an *interactive* treasure, to be personally engaged with and related to, not a gem to be stored away in a vault.

Deep down within the impossible tangles of our messy lives, we want to change for the better, but our best efforts fail to achieve satisfying results. A central theme running throughout the Bible is that our Father knows well the severity of our predicament. In loving parental response, God has come in the Person of Christ Jesus to be the means of restoring what has become so badly broken. What could be more of a treasure than God's personal involvement to bring healing for troubled hearts? To be Himself the True-North course correction for our desperate, stumbling lostness?

Becoming the Likeness of Jesus is about the treasure of transformation offered to each of us. By transformation I mean *the penetration and weaving of the Divine into the human in such a way that radical change takes place.* During His 33 years on earth, Jesus became the solution for the dilemma embedded in human hearts. A major thesis to be examined and evaluated in this book is that **Jesus continues to be the solution because what He did *for us then,* He wants to do *in us now.* The treasure of transformation is a relationship with Him and what He will do in us if we let Him.**

This book is about the dynamics of personal transformation that is at the heart of a relationship with Jesus. It is my journey and I share it openly with you, as you continue in your own search for life-changing truth. I offer this narrative in the hope that you might find something of value for your own discovery process.

The question I will explore is: Can a person undergo a transformation in which he or she actually becomes the likeness of Jesus? Such reshaping is far-removed from the way of the world *and* from the way of many churches that call themselves Christian.

In journeying within and outside of Christianity, I spent decades of my life searching for healing and truth, and have come to believe that *here-and-now* transformation is God's plan for human lives. I further believe that this transformation is entirely entwined with His ultimate intention, and that God will have His way.

PART I

A Long Day's Journey Through Night and into the Light

Chapter 1

Life Begins in a Bubble

My parents were devout Roman Catholics. Before I came along, to avoid having another child, they were practicing the rhythm method of birth control (abstaining from sex during ovulation). Times were tight economically and my father thought that two children, a boy and a girl, were enough. At the same time, my mother was secretly praying for the favor of a child. Within this ambivalence I was conceived and was born on February 4, 1942. A younger brother arrived 18 months later.

Soon after my birth, my maternal grandmother came for a visit and informed my parents that she had a dream in which it was shown to her that I had a "special destiny" in life. My parents and extended family interpreted her dream as the sure sign of a special destiny for an Irish Catholic son.

When I was two weeks old my maternal uncle, a Catholic priest, laid me on the stone altar at Holy Rosary Church in Detroit Lakes, Minnesota, dedicated me to the Blessed Virgin Mary, and proclaimed that my *special destiny* in life was to be a Catholic priest. It was a simple ritual but one that had ramifications far beyond anything anyone could have anticipated at the time.

Special but Alone

Growing up I did not have a thought of becoming anything other than a priest, and I accepted that this was my destiny. On one hand I had a sense of belonging to an elite group, a sense of having a highly valued vocation waiting for me in the future. On the other hand I had few experiences of just being a flesh-and-blood boy, belonging to a human family. All my family members and teachers knew that I would be leaving for the seminary after finishing elementary school.

Kind though my parents were, there was a reserve in them towards me. I experienced them more as guardians, taking care of me until it would be time for me to leave home after eighth grade. I felt different from everyone else; all my friends, and even my sister and two brothers seemed somewhat at arms' length. Being special had definite advantages—like receiving a deluxe tricycle with a big fur seat from a family friend who was a bishop in Kentucky—but there was also *isolation*.

I did not consciously experience the isolation, but there were recurring nightmares. I would wake up screaming in fear. My father would come into my bedroom and take me out into the hallway. Pulling up a chair, he held me in his lap until I calmed down and could return to bed. I could not really describe to my father why I was so frightened. The nightmares were different each time, but the feeling I had was the same terrifying fear.

In retrospect, it seems clear that the emotion in each recurrent nightmare was separation-anxiety generated from a lack of basic human attachment. This buried anxiety would burst through the lowered veil of consciousness during sleep, manifesting itself in fear-laced nightmares. My father physically holding me in the hallway calmed my anxiety, momentarily resolving my sense of detachment. The anxiety would abate, like stirred-up sediment in a river settling back onto a riverbed. In the morning, life would return to "normal."

While in therapy in my thirties, a psychotherapist guided me to walk consciously into one of those nightmares, and then I "got it." In the dreams I was in a transparent bubble. I could see people, animals, etc., through the bubble, but couldn't hear, smell, or touch anything. I was alone in the bubble, and the feeling that would wake me was fear. No connection, no attachment, no sense of belonging, and it was scary.

A First Arrow Goes Deep

Growing up I felt connected to my priest-destiny. There was a sense of belonging, but it was to something in the future and experientially remote. The nightmares were regular reminders of a dark side to the adventure: heroic though the journey might be, it would be lonely.

Along with being set on a purposeful path from birth, a sharp arrow was shot into my heart—an *arrow of detachment.* It was an arrow that separated me from natural human connections with people and with all the normal events a boy might have while growing up in a small Minnesota town. I was a solo-boy, and this mindset would follow me as I grew into a solo-man. In my childhood I did not think of this arrow as an enemy; it was just part of the priest-adventure, and I accepted it as such. The arrow of detachment would remain painfully buried in me for many years to come.

The Seminary: A Second Arrow Also Goes Deep

My time to leave home came after finishing Catholic elementary school in 1956. I was 14 years old. My father drove me from Detroit Lakes, Minnesota to Holy Cross Seminary in La Crosse, Wisconsin, a journey of 350 miles. I remember standing in the freshman dorm, stunned, suitcase in hand, looking out at rows of 24 single beds. On the left wall there were 12 sinks, on the right wall 24 lockers. This would be home for the next eight years.

The adventure had begun and, after the initial shock, I felt a gradual sense of belonging. This was my band of brothers with whom I could join in the high-call adventure of becoming a priest. However, the arrow of disconnection stayed firmly in place, in that we seminarians were given strict admonition against forming "particular friendships." Scripture was used to reinforce the warning. We were told that 1 Corinthians 9:22 pertained to us: to ". . . become all things to all men." As priests we would need to be servants to all members of the flock, and therefore not be attached to any person in particular. I followed the guidelines and developed a detached relationship-style.

I fully accepted my identity as a priest-to-be. This was my life. This was me. I returned home to Minnesota for vacations, but with each passing vacation, I looked more and more forward to the end of vacation, when I could return to my "real home" in the seminary.

However, upon returning to the seminary in the fall of my junior year in college (my seventh year in the seminary), I was shocked when serious doubts about my vocation suddenly surfaced. It wasn't about missing girls, or missing anything on the outside; it was more like someone had taken away a precious, shining jewel from inside of me when I wasn't looking.

I didn't know why the vocation-jewel had been removed but I no longer felt like I was destined to be a priest, and I couldn't figure out what had happened. I consulted my spiritual director and other priests, all of whom tried to dispel my doubts—to no avail. I could not retrieve my "precious gem."

I had not been taught how to talk to or listen to God in an informal, non-structured way, so He seemed silent and remote to me. I finished my senior year of college at Holy Cross, but all sense of belonging had disappeared. The jewel was gone, the adventure was over, and I was no longer a member of the band of brothers.

Once again I was a stranger in a strange land, but this time there was no future adventure waiting for me. In my perception, there was nothing waiting for me. I had to leave the seminary, and I felt a sense of shame. I had been a relatively good seminarian, but evidently something was missing. A powerful *arrow of rejection* pierced my heart but I didn't see it or feel it. It went in quickly and silently, under the radar of consciousness . . . and it went deep.

The year was 1964. I walked out of the seminary and into the world, free from the confines of the seminary. However, I was wounded and bound up with pain, fear, and anger, a fact I didn't realize or acknowledge for a long while.

Years later, when I was finally in a healing community and ready to receive healing, I discovered that I had interpreted the loss of my vocation as a belief that *God had rejected me.* I believed that *I was unworthy,* that *I wasn't qualified to advance to the major seminary* (the last four years of the twelve-year training). I had been cut from the team after my eight-year stint in the "minor leagues." Deep soul-surgery would be needed to remove this embedded belief. But for now, and for many years, I would carry the pain without an awareness of the inner, hidden interpretation that created the pain.

The seminary had been a way of life, not just a school. Gone was any sense of belonging. In a flash, my identity vanished. I was a young man stripped of a sense of purpose, and as soon as I walked outside the walls of that seminary into the world, a cavernous sinkhole opened up inside of me.

When I left the seminary at age 21, I had developed into a thoroughly self-centered person, a state that would stubbornly stay in place for the next 20 years. However well-intentioned the nuns and priests might have been in my elementary, high school, and college education, I walked out of Holy Cross Seminary in 1964 as an insulated, isolated, narrow-minded man. And, characteristic of pride, I was so bound up into myself that I couldn't see my true condition. I thought I was doing fine.

That false sense of complacency would be severely challenged, and eventually shredded, in the years to come.

Chapter 2

Journeys into and out of Darkness

The next 20 years can be characterized as multiple attempts to break out of "the bubble." These attempts cascaded from one upheaval to another, sometimes spilling from one worldview into another, from one career dead-end into a hopeful new direction . . . only to result in yet another complete swap-out because the new light dimmed, or ended in complete darkness.

This book is about changes and exchanges that bring about transformation; in my case that would necessitate an emergence from my cocoon-bubble. The following summary of life-events documents a succession of shifts, reconstructions, and exchanges that did not result in substantial change—I didn't break out of the bubble. As such, this is my experience of what transformation is *not*. In Chapter 3, the gears will shift into what I began to experience as real transformation.

A Dull Ache

Upon leaving the seminary, I entered Marquette University in Milwaukee, Wisconsin and earned a Master's degree in Theology. My intention was to become a non-ordained lay theologian. In the seminary, and continuing at Marquette, God-talk filled classes, retreats, and sermons. There seemed to be a mysterious kind of assumption in play—that somehow we were making God present by *talking* about Him. At Marquette the God-talk was accelerated to the next level because *all* the courses were about Him.

I don't know if I thought that ideas about God would somehow make their way down into my heart and out into my life, changing me perhaps in an osmosis-type process. But *knowing about* a loving God did not translate into a loving relationship with God or with others.

I can remember feeling holy and godly because I was spending most of my time talking about God, though I didn't lead a godly life. I didn't have a clue that this was exactly why Jesus rebuked the Pharisees: they were involved not with the *living God* but with concepts, laws, and doctrines *about* God.

I was living in my head and barely realized the state I was in. My heart was so disconnected from my life that I could not feel the hunger and thirst for real life that would later emerge. I just felt a dull ache.

The Death of a Worldview

After receiving my Master's degree at Marquette, I taught theology for two years—the first year at Portland University in Oregon, and then a year at Santa Clara University in California. In between those two years I married a woman who had also gone through Marquette's degree program in theology.

I hadn't dated much, certainly not enough to open my locked-up heart, but at age twenty-five I thought it was time to marry. However, my solo-structured soul was ill-equipped for relational intimacy; nothing but relational pain, for my wife and for me, emerged from this marriage.

Taking leading thoughts from the liberal theology taught at Marquette, I began to explore the many challenges to Christian orthodoxy that were developing in the years after the seemingly progressive Second Vatican Council ended in 1964. I wedged my mind into the cracks that began to appear in orthodox doctrines, moral codes, and understandings of God. Slowly but surely I tuned out the corruption within myself. The word *sin* gradually disappeared from my everyday vocabulary and from my teaching.

During my brief teaching career at Portland and Santa Clara, my rock-hard Catholic worldview began to crumble, and like a prisoner clawing through the rubble of prison walls shaken apart by an earthquake, I was intent on escape.[1] In my experience, Jesus had

---

[1] A reminder that I am describing only *my* experience of Catholicism.

been a dogma-Jesus, and a ritual-Jesus rather than a living God. When the dogmas and rituals crumbled, and when I believed that I no longer needed a Savior, it was apparent that I hadn't developed a personal relationship with Jesus.

Before the end of my second year of teaching, I had discarded Catholicism—indeed, the entire worldview of Christianity was dissipating within my soul. I began to feel a dreadful emptiness inside.

Without clear lines of demarcation between good and evil, it was amazing how easy it was to slide into a grey, shapeless void where everything was relative and neutral. However, nature abhors a vacuum, and a powerful replacement would soon arrive, filling the void—and I was a sponge ready to absorb.

The Rise of the Self

Without much forethought, I resigned my position at Santa Clara University and enrolled in a Master's degree program in Social Work at San Diego State University in Southern California. By the end of my first year at San Diego State, the void was filled by an immersion into the psychologies of Carl Rogers, Abraham Maslow, Albert Ellis, and many others who had developed the theme of *self-actualization*. For someone who inwardly felt that his *self* had been hijacked since birth, these were initially very refreshing waters to swim in.

I filled my freshly vacated mind with these "liberating" ideas. Self-realization and self-actualization replaced the need for salvation. Catholicism had been poured into me; I had taken it in but never really wrestled with it or willingly *chose* it. It was not difficult, at least consciously, to let all the doctrines drain out and be replaced with a psychology that seemed to be healing and life-giving.

Some of my new classmates did drugs, and I indulged in the pursuit of "freedom" through chemicals. I took mescaline on several occasions and smoked marijuana on a regular basis. Expanding my consciousness through drugs seemed compatible with the new doctrine of self-actualization. At age 26 I had become a late-blooming hippie. I let my hair and beard grow long, wore a wrinkled Army-surplus jacket, and was stoned much of the time—or speeding high on amphetamines so I could stay up all night to finish term papers at school.

A basic tenet in my psychology classes was that human nature is inherently good. *Evil* is anything that frustrates or hampers our essential self-actualizing nature—such as antiquated traditions, controlling governmental or religious authority, and absolute moral norms.

I adopted the belief that it was fine to be self-focused, supposedly inching ever closer to the prize of self-actualization. My internalized mantra became: *Just let folks self-actualize and all problems will resolve themselves because of human innate goodness.*

I had no idea that I was embracing a *self* that one day I would discover had been nailed to a cross.

For now my optimistic belief was succinctly summed up in *The Humanist Manifesto*: "Man is at last becoming aware that he alone is responsible for the realization of the world of his dreams, that he has within himself the power for its achievement . . . . While there is much that we do not know, humans are responsible for what we are or will become. No deity will save us; we must save ourselves."

By the end of my two years in San Diego, I had substantially dropped out of mainstream America, heeding drug-guru Timothy Leary's advice to "turn on, tune in, and drop out." I was still a part of "the system" in that I had a Master's degree in Social Work and had accepted a job in the Napa County Department of Social Services in northern California. In summary:

- I had replaced the religion of Christianity with the religion of Humanism (though at the time I did not think of it as a religion).
- Through drugs my mind had been altered and my perceptions were supposedly lining up with "reality."
- To complete this version of out-with-the-old and in-with-the-new, my marriage ended after less than two years and no children. Promiscuity filled that empty space, and I thought of the new relationships as just more positive steps towards self-actualization.

There were also some unpleasant changes. When relationships would end (and especially if rejection was involved), it would tap into the reservoir of pain hidden in my heart. Powerful emotions of anger, sadness, and fear would well up. Anxiety from a life-long lack of human attachment and pain from my "rejection" in the seminary rippled out into my soul—like waves from stones that had been thrown into the pond of my life years ago.

In the safety of a humanistic psychologist's office, I began to uncover the seething turmoil underneath the surface. But the therapists I saw only dealt with the immediate pain and not the deeper issues, or they provided *insight* into the issues but not *healing.* So I would get patched up and then move along to the next adventure. In 1970, after graduating from San Diego State University, the next adventure was Napa, California.

Another Dream Dies

Napa hit me smack in the face with a part of life I had not seen. Along with a classmate from San Diego, I was hired by Napa County to open a Child Protection Services unit. My tidy world of self-realization, expanding consciousness, and opening my "doors of perception" was soberly shaken by the reality of an alcoholic father putting out lit cigarettes on his three-year-old son's back, by parents punching and kicking their children into submission, and by the horrors of child sexual abuse.

Day after day I witnessed this dark side of life, and the tools in my clinical toolbox were woefully inadequate to deal with any of it. I used what I was taught, applying soul-bandages here and there, and "managing" situations to prevent further damage from occurring. But after a year, I was totally discouraged.

There was tremendous confusion inside of me. In San Diego I had been taught in the classroom that self-actualization could be achieved without much conflict, and that the intrinsic goodness of the human self would come through once people saw the truth of innate human goodness. However, in real-life Napa, the degree of dysfunction that I experienced in the abuse and the broken relationships was far beyond the parameters of my academic training and experience.

In my clients in Napa, I witnessed extensive self-hatred, low self-esteem, despair, and hopelessness, among other maladies of the soul. I intuitively knew that the evil I encountered was not coming solely from external forces such as authoritarian government, a restrictive moral code, or bad parenting. This dark stuff was seeping out from deep inside the souls of the many persons I encountered. Within just a few months, my humanistic/hippie understanding of life was on very shaky ground.

There was another complicating reality that caught me by surprise. My own unresolved pain, anger, and anxiety were triggered and brought to the surface by exposure to daily doses of unresolved relational turmoil in the lives of my clients. The net effect of this triggering was a gradual amplification of *my* inner turmoil, heading towards a breaking point.

During that year in Napa, I increasingly felt as though I was inside a room in which all four walls were slowly but inexorably closing in on me. I was slowly being smothered and crushed. The force crushing me was not just what was happening in Napa. The situation there somehow touched into the whole edifice of my biography. I had replaced and exchanged many ideas and beliefs during my years in Santa Clara and San Diego, but the foundational structures upon which my early life had been built were not so easily dislodged.

It felt as though the enclosing walls were composed of my whole life, from birth on. All the formative forces seemed to be there as bricks in the walls. Up to this point in Napa, none of my exchanges had dealt with these "bricks." It seemed as though the whole structure was still there on the inside, closing in on me.

An urgent plan came together in my mind: *To run far away . . . to somehow step outside of everything I had ever been part of since birth.* This took the form of selling my 1967 Ford Mustang to raise money for a trip abroad. I had no idea how long I would be gone or if I would return. It was the strongest urgency I had felt in my short life and I moved with it. Given my disillusion with humanistic psychology and the inner walls closing in on me, fleeing seemed my only choice.

I had never felt so fearfully lost, and in that moment I had no compass, no anchor, no sense of direction whatsoever. Embarking on a journey wasn't just about getting away for a while. It seemed that the entirety of my old life was failing and collapsing. I wanted to shed this old life and exchange it for a new one. In the hippie jargon of the day, I was setting out *to find myself*.

A Trip Abroad

Finding myself first meant *losing myself*, i.e., disconnecting from everything in my life up to this point. I put my plan into action in 1971 by flying (a one-way ticket) from New York to Luxembourg. I hitch-hiked throughout Europe, into North Africa, and back to Europe. In Paris, I secured visas and supplies for an overland journey to India.

From Paris I hitch-hiked to Italy, crossed over to Greece by ship, and then made the long trek to India by hitch-hiking through Turkey, Iran, Afghanistan, and Pakistan. I lived in India for eight months, experiencing a culture very different than the American way of life. I remember being emotionally overwhelmed by many encounters with death—daily seeing people dying on the streets or seeing corpses burning on pyres located along the banks of the Ganges River, where I rented a one-room hut. There was a close encounter with my own mortality in that I was sick much of the time. I sought medical help and began to recover, but I was ready to leave India.

I returned to Europe to recuperate. After a few months in Switzerland I toured the Scandinavian countries, made a one-week trip to Ireland, and finally returned to the United States towards the end of 1973. I was saturated and weary with travel. The United States felt like a long-lost home and I wanted to return, though I had no sense of direction or purpose.

Dozing Divinity

One particular influence warrants mention here. Although much of my wandering abroad was aimless, as a late-blooming hippie I moved within communities of like-minded people—of which there were many in the early 1970s. Part of "getting lost" was stripping away any connection to *religion*, but while traveling I began to take an interest in a new worldview that permeated much of my hippie culture.

By many popular proponents of astrology, Earth had entered the Age of Aquarius sometime in the 19th century. Since an astrological age is about 2,160 years long, by 1971 Earth was just getting started in this *New Age*. The astrological sign of Aquarius is a man pouring spiritual water out of a large vessel. The in vogue interpretation of this sign was that the hallmark of the Age of Aquarius would be an outpouring of truth and an expansion of consciousness. This would be the Age in which mankind would take control of its own destiny, evolving into its rightful divine heritage.

The basic beliefs of this New Age worldview can be summarized as follows: *We are all Divine. We are God, we just don't know it yet. What we call God is everywhere, in everyone and everything. We search all over the world* (as I was doing) *and right there, already inside us is this dozing Divinity, waiting to be discovered and awakened.*

New Age spirituality planted itself into my wandering soul and took root. For awhile I felt on track to truth and freedom. I stopped doing drugs and strove to overcome my ego and ascend into the Divine realm, the "Higher Self."

While in India I spent time in the ashram of an Indian guru. I learned and practiced several meditation techniques, trying to see down into my "Divinity" with my spiritual "third eye." Back in Europe I also studied and practiced other forms of spirituality.

After returning to the United States in 1973, I spent my first months back with my family of origin in Minnesota, but I was restless and wanted to leave soon after arriving. I had absorbed and practiced New Age beliefs, but they had not brought peace. The pre-travel panic feelings were gone, and that was a relief, but I still felt deeply unsettled.

A Second Trip Abroad

Returning to Napa seemed my next step, not because I had any sense of direction but because Napa had been my jumping off point three years prior. In Napa, I tumbled from one loose end to another until connecting with a "Spiritual Science" community in the nearby city of Sacramento, California. I moved there and felt myself drawn into what I thought of as another variation of a New Age community.

The restless feeling began to dissipate as I became more involved in the life of the community formed around the teachings of an Austrian clairvoyant named Rudolf Steiner. My interest in their curriculum for spiritual counseling turned into another three-year journey of study (1977-1980), this time to their Emerson College in Sussex, England.

After returning to the United States from Emerson College in 1980, I spent three more years in Spiritual Science communities in New Hampshire and Michigan, living and learning via the writings of Rudolf Steiner.

I had resumed my quest for truth by trying to develop my inner spiritual faculties so I could achieve what was called *Knowledge of Higher Worlds*. But, while in Detroit, Michigan, my interest in Steiner's clairvoyant knowledge began to wane . . . another light that had begun bright and then dimmed with time. His 30 books and 6000 lectures had lost their sheen and had become to me dark and dull.

More Lost than Ever

In 1984, living in Detroit, my status consisted of the following:

- I had plunged into and out of a second marriage and now had a son. I had married an English woman whom I had met at Emerson College. I walked out of this second marriage much as I had walked out of my first marriage. Before long I had taken up with a woman and her three children.
- Enrolling in a doctoral program in clinical psychology, I discovered that many of my former mentors in humanistic

psychology had moved beyond humanism (which they now described as a narrow, restrictive view of self-actualization). They had embraced New Age spirituality and declared that *real* self-actualization involved merging with the *Higher Self*. Shedding their humanistic views, they had become enlightened "transpersonal psychologists." I read their new books, picked up the new drumbeat, and began following in their footsteps.

- I had resumed smoking marijuana on an occasional basis, trying to tranquilize the constant current of anxiety in my soul. Meditation and other spiritual practices had not calmed the troubled waters rippling through me since childhood.

After all my study, striving, practicing meditation, and pursuing spiritually-based healing methods, no real transformation had taken place. At the Centre for Transpersonal Psychology in London, a therapist had guided me into bringing my childhood nightmares into conscious awareness. But *understanding* what was going on in the nightmares neither removed the fear nor removed me from "the bubble." I could not will myself out of it. I was still locked up inside myself, in a bubble of isolation.

Relationship-wise my life was a disaster. I had gone from one relationship to another, from one marriage to another, subconsciously trying to remove the deep *arrow of detachment* from my childhood. I kept trying to attach, to belong, to be close to someone. Having a *situation-ethics* code of morality (everything is relative . . . no absolutes) allowed me to begin and end sexual relationships at will, but such license had led neither to freedom nor to peace.

Bumbling in and out of relationships, I was now headed towards my third marriage, hoping somewhere in my heart that this would be the one to heal my detachment wound and set me free.

In short, my life was a mess. My journeys to *find myself* were journeys to nowhere. I did not acknowledge it as such but I was treading water, hanging on, hoping that my involvements in a new relationship and a new career would get me up and swimming. Life had become more complicated than ever before, with new and growing family responsibilities added to the mix. Weariness intensified as I continued treading water.

Chapter 3

Real Life Begins

In late autumn of 1984, in a suburb of Detroit, Michigan. I had accepted an invitation to attend a church service, more out of curiosity than anything else,

I remember well that Wednesday evening service in Brightmoor Tabernacle, an Assemblies of God church. I had never been in a Protestant church before, so at first I felt strange sitting there in the pew, faintly feeling the reprimand my parents would have given for attending a Protestant church. However, those feelings were quickly dispelled as the pastor launched into the Last Supper discourse from the Gospel of John.

I had heard many sermons in my life but nothing like this one. The pastor skillfully opened up passage after passage, letting the theme of God's love for us exude from the verses like a delicate fragrance. In those moments I was touched on the inside by something that imperceptibly made its way past my protective walls and defenses.

The sermon was not a transmission of knowledge from the pastor's head to my head. His words were coming from his *heart* and I felt energized and enlivened in *my* heart. Driving home that evening, I realized that I had just heard the best sermon of my life.

I returned on Sunday for the full service. Although my curiosity was piqued by Wednesday's sermon, I was still wary of being in a Protestant church. My usual mindset had settled back into a defensive, critical mode, and skeptically I watched about 500 people talking in the aisles and beginning to fill the pews. I felt as though I was on the *inside* of reality, and these church folks were on the *outside*, in some weird, surreal, religious world.

The service began. Within ten minutes, in an utterly surprising shift, my perception completely flipped: *They* were on the inside of something I intuitively felt was real and alive, and *I* was on the outside. In that moment, at age 42, I had my first authentic encounter with God.

I heard a clearly authoritative, yet gentle voice say, "I am life." I did not hear the voice audibly with my ears, yet I somehow perceived the words within me, and they were being spoken by a person. I had a sense of a *personal presence* other than myself. It was not the voice of my self-talk chattering away as it did throughout the day. This presence was clearly distinct from myself, yet communicating with me.

As those words were spoken, a remarkable thing happened within me. Like a fog lifting, I saw that everything I was attached to—the drugs, the hippie lifestyle, my New Age beliefs, my frantic search for knowledge—all comprised an extensive life-support "machine" into which I was plugged. I could see and feel the tangled tubes attaching me to those things, and I saw that this whole life-support system was really *pseudo-life*.

Then a gentle but firm understanding came into my mind: *You must choose what to have as life—Me or the life-supports to which you are attached.* The tone and meaning of the proposal were crystal clear: it was an invitation, and I somehow sensed that this was a God-invitation. But it was a one-or-the-other proposition; I could not have it both ways. I had to choose what would be *life* for me. There was a startled pause as I absorbed this realization. Then, inwardly I said, "I choose You."

At that time I didn't know what name would describe Whom I had encountered: God, Creator, Ultimate Reality, Father, Holy Spirit, Jesus, The Source, or Life, as in the "I am Life." C.S. Lewis sometimes referred to God as "The Real," and there in Brightmoor Tabernacle such a name made sense.

I had been shown that I was living in unreality and calling it reality. My entire perception had been flipped and reversed. With different eyes I watched the people singing and praying during the rest of the Sunday service. They were not religious nuts playing church and going through mechanical motions. I could see that they were experiencing something real and they knew it. They were alive with *real life*.

I did not obey the inner impulse I felt, but it was clearly there in me—to bow down to the Person who spoke to me, who was in this church and involved with these people. I was in the presence of an awesome Being, yet this Being was personal and inviting.

At the time, I did not respond fully to the invitation, but I took a first step in a long journey by going home and throwing away all my marijuana and its paraphernalia. That drug had been my major "life-support"; disconnecting from it in a radical way was a major step.

Below the Surface

It didn't happen magically or immediately, but a new dynamic was set into motion by the perceptible presence of a Person who invited me to step into *Life*. I felt a glimpse of hope. Yes, over the years I had pursued several seemingly bright lights that had dimmed and then darkened. There were so many relationship-failures, so many "identities" begun and ended, so many hopes and dreams that had vaporized, so many dead ends.

Several times previously, in my search for truth, I had been deceived by counterfeits that promised healing, wholeness, and peace. Only the desire to know real truth kept pulling me forward from the dead-ends and failures of my many searches. I began to look into this new light to see if it was *real* light. I began to engage with this Person who claimed to be Life. I wanted to discover *whether or not this Life was real*.

I strongly sensed that the Person I had encountered in Brightmoor Tabernacle was the God of the Bible, and after a preparatory class I accepted the Gospel of Jesus Christ and was baptized, full-immersion style. I didn't hesitate to move forward quickly because it didn't feel like a re-entry into the *religion* of Christianity. I had an uncanny sense of entering a new dimension; I was drawn to a God who wanted to engage personally.

After moving to North Carolina in 1986, a seismic shift of consciousness shook my world. As the numbing of my "life-support system" wore off, and as New Age spirituality lost its deceptive sheen, an unnerving truth was about to emerge.

While attending a church in the town of Chapel Hill, at the direction of some men who were mentoring me, I fasted and prayed for over two weeks, consuming only fluids. Afterwards I met with the men and they asked me what God had shown me during these weeks. I began to tell them my life-story, and at the end, through my disclosure and their comments, I experienced a staggering conviction of the depth of my self-centeredness.

It was like looking below the surface of a huge iceberg to encompass its true size. What I saw was overwhelmingly massive. I broke down into tears for a long time, confronted soberly by the pervasiveness of my pride, arrogance, and sense of entitlement. I cringed at what I saw of the judgmental, lustful, petty, impatient, utterly selfish state of my soul.

I felt helpless. In that moment, like none before, I knew I needed a Savior. The name *Jesus* made complete sense to me, beyond what I had experienced in Michigan. I now knew who Jesus is at a deeper level than before, and I knew how desperately I needed Him.

As a humanistic psychologist, I had thrown out the word *sin* along with my old theology books. As a New Ager, I had cleverly disguised evil as *ignorance* that could be corrected by *enlightened knowledge*. But in that moment with those men, and in many moments following that event, I began to sense the reality of evil in the world, especially up close and personal—in me.

Looking below the surface of my heart and seeing such corruption, I began to soberly realize how deeply rooted was my sense of *self-ownership*. For decades, I had fought fiercely for my "independence" and now, initially, I balked at the thought of fully trusting or relying on anyone, even a Person who said *I am Life*. For many years, *self* had been my only master.

As the rationalizations for my pervasive self-focus began to wear off and be exposed, I became more willing to look at my self-life and see its true character: resentful, fussy, greedy, haughty, touchy, vain . . . blind to everything except its own gratification.

However, I did not grasp or accept the necessity of this old self to die. *Crucified* is a "*hard* word," as the Irish say. My *self* had been pumped up and had been running the show for many years; it was not inclined to submit to purposes beyond itself. Further, I had no sense of *how* to shift out of this self-focus, supposing it to be something that *I* had to do. It wasn't at all clear how my character and personality could change.

Note on the Role of Choice

In Brightmoor Tabernacle, when I said "I choose You," it was my choice; but in my guarded, critical, selfish little self, I don't think I was capable of so grand and life-changing a decision on my own.

God's sovereignty and the gift of human choice are still mysterious to me, as to how they interweave in human lives. Something happened that day in Brightmoor Tabernacle, and it was clearly God's favor setting the scene; and my response of *yes* to God's invitation was also part of the equation.

Both Favor and human choice were factors, and a deed was done that day which would change my life forever. The prophecy of Zachariah, recorded in the Gospel of Luke 1:78-79, was activated in the soul of a man named William Day when he was 42 years old:

". . . Through the tender mercy of our God,
With which the Dawn
from on high has broken upon us;
To give light to those who sit in darkness and the shadow of death,
To guide our feet into the way of peace."

Chapter 4

Real Healing

While living in North Carolina, I worked in a mental health center and then a smoking cessation clinic. I finished my dissertation and received a PhD in Clinical Psychology in 1987, and gradually shifted towards a more spiritual understanding of healing. I began networking in Christian counseling circles, meeting many counselors and pastors in the area, and even began seeing patients privately in a home-office. I read books on Christian counseling, listened to audio tapes, and attended seminars. Finally I landed a job in a Christian counseling clinic.

What I encountered in the field of Christian counseling was basically the same cognitive therapy of my secular training in psychotherapy. Secular therapy focused on positive thoughts of succeeding and how to manage behavior. Christian counseling simply added into the cognitive mix thoughts from the Bible that focused on God's goodness, provision, and love.

The Scriptures were rich and deep, such as "Be transformed by the renewing of your mind" (Romans 12:2), and ". . . it is no longer I who live but Christ lives in me" (Galatians 2:20), suggesting significant and thorough change. However, for the most part, the therapeutic approach of Christian counseling focused almost solely on *immediate consciousness*, the top layer of the mind. The hidden issues in the heart were seldom addressed.

From God's Word it seemed clear to me that all humans have darkened depths and hidden anxieties which need to be searched out and exposed by God (Psalm 139:23). Yet, most of what I learned and tried to apply from Christian counseling methods were concepts, principles, and coping strategies . . . all in the form of the counselor downloading Bible verses and advice from his or her mind into the mind of the client.

NOT WHAT LED TO BILLS
TRANSFORMATION ON PAGE 19

I was a rookie Christian counselor and went with the flow of traditional methods. Even though Jesus said "I am the truth" (John 14:6), in the initial methods I learned and practiced, the operative principle was: *truth = true information.*

The rationale seemed to be that if clients, indeed all Christians, could *push* the right thoughts into their minds, the power of these holy thoughts would shove the negative, false, sinful thoughts out.[2] Strategies that I used on myself and on patients included repetition, exhortation, and rebuking.

Counselor advice might include repetition of Bible verses over and over for a month, or putting these verses on 3"x5" cards on a bathroom mirror as constant reminders—trying to *pound in* the new knowledge and flood the mind. I heard pastors shouting out phrases such as "God loves you!" from the pulpit, as though the force of an elevated decibel level might drive the truth below the surface-waters of the mind. *POWER AND CONTROL—DECEPTION*

In 1993, my private practice as a full-time Christian counselor began in a basement office given to me by the Fellowship of Christ, an Evangelical Presbyterian Church in the town of Cary, North Carolina. My counseling style focused on trying to implant Biblically based thoughts into patients about how God sees them. I hoped that these thoughts would *override* self-defeating thoughts that kept people chained to negative emotions and unwanted behavior. I was practicing Christian cognitive therapy. *NOT THE PROCESS THAT INITIALLY WORKS OF FREE BILL*

As a counselor, I thought it was my job to be a storehouse of Bible verses, stress management strategies, addiction-breaking secrets, and other information that I could download into my patients' minds to make them well. Some of my patients knew the Bible better than I did, but they were hoping I could help them move the truth that they knew in their *heads* to their *hearts* and then into their *behavior.*

The shared understanding among my colleagues was that there was an invisible barrier between head and heart that needed to be penetrated; hence the aforementioned methods of taping Bible

---

[2] I do not discount the power of the Holy Spirit to penetrate deeply. This will be clarified later.

verses onto the bathroom mirror and listening to sermons over and over on audio tapes. It was generally accepted in my profession that our main problems were in the hidden regions of the heart, but the dilemma was how to get in there.

Similar to my New Age psychological training, there seemed to be an implicit belief that if a person could only grasp the *correct knowledge* in his or her mind, then healing would somehow happen. This is like receiving a diagnosis of having a malignant tumor in your body and believing that a cure will now magically occur because you correctly understand the diagnosis. **But there is another step needed: the tumor must be removed.**

I didn't comprehend this at the time, but a "surgical procedure" is sometimes necessary in the *soul*, and such a surgery requires the skill of the Master Surgeon. However, in the therapeutic process conducted by myself and my colleagues, God had, at best, only a minor role.

We Christian counselors would enlist the blessings of the Holy Spirit at the beginning of the counseling session, then relegate Him to the role of a silent bystander and witness. At the end of the session we would call on Him to close the meeting.

I fell into this same pattern, even though I knew with my head-knowledge that **the Holy Spirit was called Counselor, Healer, Comforter, and the Light who searches darkened regions of hearts to show truthfully what is going on there. Further, I knew that He is a Person who can communicate with us in any moment and bring to bear His power to heal.** But we were not tapping into the Holy Spirit as the primary source of healing.

Not yet in Gear

Some change and healing occurred in me and in my patients, but it was more symptom-reduction than real healing; more managing and coping than healing-at-the-core; more tentative improvement and adjustment to circumstances than actual transformation. I didn't realize it at the time, but what was missing was the action of replacing old thought-patterns that were settled into regions of the

[handwritten margin note: And many Christian leaders still do...]

mind deeper than immediate consciousness. What would become clear later is the necessity to *remove* and *replace* dysfunctional beliefs, not try to shove them aside.

Up to this point, in the early 1990s, I had neither the understanding nor the skill to remove old interpretations and beliefs. I didn't realize it but soul-surgery was needed, not palliative care. But I had not yet met a Christian counselor or pastor who had expertise in spiritual-surgery.

The truth was right there in Scripture. Jesus gave hints about *removing the old and replacing* it with the new, as in His image of putting new wine into new wine skins. He did not shove anything aside; He replaced it, made it new—a *new creation* (2 Corinthians 5:17). Wasn't the mission of Jesus to substitute and exchange at the deepest levels of our being (2 Corinthians 5:21). And didn't Jesus tell us that the Holy Spirit would be directly and personally involved in showing us all truth (John 16:13)? His truth was there in plain sight, but I didn't take hold of it.

And then, in 1995, along came Nancy.

The woman walked slowly into my office and slumped down into a chair, her first statement a heavy sigh. Nancy was a pleasant-looking woman in her mid-forties, but her complexion was pale and she carried heavy weariness in her eyes and shoulders. I wondered how long she had been so burdened, months certainly, maybe years. Her husband, Tom, came in behind her and took a chair slightly off to the side. He had a quiet demeanor and looked at his wife as though he were her bodyguard. The focus was clearly on her.

Nancy began her story by recounting an event that had happened eight months previously, while driving to meet a client. She was an interior decorator, working in the Raleigh, NC area for the past several years. Suddenly, without warning, she felt grabbed by a panic attack: intense fear, pounding heart, shaking, shortness of breath, and sweating. Dizziness and fear seized her and she felt that she was about to go crazy, or even die. She pulled off the road shortly after the attack began, and when it passed she caught her breath and returned to work, though badly shaken by the event.

Nancy shifted nervously in her chair as she proceeded to tell me that several more panic attacks occurred over the next six weeks. She would have fear of having an attack, and that would bring on another attack. She also had intermittent anxiety unrelated to anything except the anticipation of having another panic attack.

The weariness I saw, in her eyes and her body language, was from fighting fear. She was worn out from the struggle and was just waiting for the next time the claws of fear would jump out and grab her again. She was still having occasional panic attacks.

During the weeks after the first panic attack, Nancy had sought help from a psychiatrist and a psychotherapist, and she told me about the two medications she was currently taking. The medications had slowed down the frequency of the attacks, but the undercurrent of anxiety was always there. The psychotherapy did not seem to be helping.

She had heard about me from a friend who had been a patient of mine. Nancy said she did not know if her problem had any spiritual basis, but she was a Christian and wanted a Christian counselor. She added that she was very desperate and knew she needed God's power to get through what had become the crisis of her life.

She had quit her job and had become a recluse, sitting at home with the curtains closed. She could not drive anymore. Her husband, an avid fisherman, enjoyed going to the coast on fishing trips. However, she could not tolerate him being more than 50 miles away without having a wave of anxiety. She said she felt sad that he couldn't go fishing any more. Her husband spoke up to say that he was willingly sacrificing his hobby; he just wanted her to get well. Though they did not say so, I guessed this crisis was a strain on their marriage. There was heaviness in the air.

Both Nancy and Tom were carrying heavy burdens and had showed up at my doorstep for help. What could I offer that would be effective and healing? An alleviation of symptoms would not do here, and I began to feel a burden myself. For some time I had thought that fear was a spiritual problem, so I agreed to walk into that darkness with them.

"Nothing is too big for God," I said. I could hear the uncertainty in my voice and wondered if they could hear it as well. Evidently those were the words she wanted to hear. She smiled weakly and said she would like to begin treatment with me. We set up an appointment for the following week. Slowly they got up from their chairs and we said good-bye.

On the day of her next appointment, Nancy returned to my office looking about the same as she had the week before. I turned from my desk and rolled my chair around to face her. Her husband once again sat off to the side, watching.

I began by asking Nancy to start telling the story of her life, from the beginning. In my therapy practice I used autobiography as a primary way to dig below the surface into the deeper issues of one's life. I clarified for Nancy that I was not asking her to give me background information. Rather, I was asking her to tell her life-story, year by year, chapter by chapter. We would listen together and try to hear the underlying themes, motifs, recurrent threads—bringing the story right up to the present day.

Nancy began describing a chaotic childhood with an early breakup between her mother and father. After Nancy's father exited, she lived with her mother, whom she described as having a serious alcohol problem coupled with significant mental health issues. She recounted an early memory at age four, in which she was standing outside the front door of a house, suitcase by her side, watching her mother walk away and then drive off. Her mother was evidently unable to cope with her problems and also raise Nancy, so she gave her away to her childless sister and brother-in-law who lived in another town.

Nancy then described the ranch-style house of her aunt and uncle. Their bedroom was at one end of the house and Nancy's at the other end. I asked her to describe what life was like, living with them in their home. She said they were stern, not warm folks. As an example, she told of having to sleep in her bedroom without having any light, even from the nearby bathroom. Despite Nancy's repeated pleas, her aunt and uncle would not relent.

She said, "I have memories of lying in my bed, covers pulled up to my chin, just scared to death." At this point in the session, she closed her eyes without any direction from me, perhaps because the memory was so strong and vivid.

I asked, "Were you alone there?" "Yes," she said. "My aunt and uncle were either in the living room or had gone to bed. I didn't know which because they always closed my door."

What happened next will sound odd to your ears, as it did to mine. "Was anyone else there?" I asked. I immediately felt foolish. Nancy had just told me she was alone. Why did I ask such a dumb question? At that time in my life I had few spiritual thoughts about God's omnipresence and that He would be there; I was not fishing for that response.

"No one, I was alone."

My self-talk was, *Move on with her story, Bill, she said she was alone and feeling very afraid.*

I was about to push on into having her describe more of her life in that home, when, still with eyes closed, she said, "Oh . . . God was there!" Her face brightened as she was seeing something happen in the memory. "The whole room is filled with light and Jesus is standing next to my bed. I know it is Him." Moments passed. "He is touching my arm and telling me that He loves me and that He'll always be with me and take care of me."

We stayed in that memory for a while, both of us soaking in what was happening. "All the fear is gone," she finally said. "All the fear is gone and I just feel so peaceful."

I looked over at Tom. He was also absorbing what was taking place. No longer watching from the sideline, he looked to be very engaged and drawn into what was occurring, though his eyes had a startled look.

I did not know what to do next. Nancy opened her eyes and began to weep copious tears of relief and joy. It was as though the person before me had been released from a dark dungeon. She was overcome with the emotion of gaining freedom after long years of living in the grip of fear. Her tears were those of release and freedom.

Coming out of my own absorption in this scene, my mind slowly cleared. I focused and then like the sharp peal of a bell going off in my brain, I astutely knew what to do next . . . I handed Nancy a box of

Kleenex. That was easily the most significant contribution I made to the proceedings that day.

We drew the session to a close and set up another appointment for the following week. Nancy and Tom had much to absorb, as did I. Somehow I knew that things would never be the same for them, or for me. Real healing had begun for her, and real training had begun for me.

When Nancy and Tom returned the following week, I began by asking her how she was doing. Although a habituated heaviness and weariness were still present in much of her body language, there was light in her eyes and new energy in her voice.

She first said that the memory of being alone at night in the darkened bedroom had changed. She still had a sense of Jesus' presence there and the room was filled with light. Several times she had tried in her mind to make the bedroom dark again, but she could not. And she added that the fear was still completely gone. The three of us exchanged words of amazement and then resumed the process of Nancy telling her life-story.

The Rest of the Story

As you might imagine, Nancy had lots of anxiety and fear growing up. Rejection and abandonment created a sense of isolation, and she always felt on the outside looking in. Her sense of self-confidence and self-worth were very low, and she found her way into peer groups in which the members also saw themselves as outsiders. She had not gone off the deep end into drugs and promiscuity, but in her younger years she found alcohol and food to be useful pain relievers and comforters.

Early on in their marriage, she and her husband had joined a church. Both of them became involved in church activities and services, but she always felt an emotional distance from God. She tried to please Him by behaving well, though when she failed she always felt anxious and guilty for having disappointed Him.

During the next six weeks of treatment, unusual and unprecedented healing occurred. Nancy did not again have a visual manifestation of

Jesus in her memories, but she felt a sense of His Presence seep into her memories as she continued telling her story. It was as though His Presence flashed through her whole life from the initial blast of Light in the bedroom memory.

For example, she would be describing a scene in adolescence, talking about how lonely and dejected she felt . . . and then she would interject, "Oh, but Jesus was there." She would pause for a few moments, letting that thought enter the memory, and the feelings in the memory would change from negative to positive feelings of peace.

I did not pull out my 3"x5" cards and write Scripture verses for her to read and repeat. She simply let the presence of the Lord come into each event in her life as she recounted it. He dissolved the anxiety, boosted her fragile self-image, and removed the doubts about her prospects for the future. I was watching someone come alive before my eyes as we progressed year by year, up to the present.

She experienced being *loved* rather than being *rejected*, and being *valued* instead of being *outcast*. It was a swap-out, an exchanged-life process that was actual, not merely conceptual. **There was no therapeutic task of getting truth or positive thoughts from her head to her heart. As I saw it, she had opened her simple faith to acknowledge the truth that God was in that bedroom with her.** He walked right in through the open portal of her faith, and from there He entered any soul-room (memory) in which she came to the door and said, "Come in."

As the weeks went by and as I listened to her, I often thought of the passage in Revelation 3:20 NIV: "Here I am! I stand at the door and knock. If anyone hears My voice and opens the door, I will come in to him and eat with him, and he with Me." Nancy heard Jesus' voice, kept opening doors for Him to come in, and eagerly savored the delicious meal of His Presence.

Within three months, and after 9 or 10 therapy sessions, Nancy had discontinued all of her medications without any severe withdrawal symptoms.[3] She had no more panic attacks. She returned to her work, driving there herself. The last time she came to my office, she came without her husband and looked like a different person. The weary look, the forlorn voice, and the shuffling gait were gone. She was full of life and energy, and light beamed from her eyes.

At the end of the session, we agreed that she would call me on an as-needed basis. As she went through the doorway of my office, she turned around and said, "Tom has gone back to his fishing at the coast." She smiled, turned and left. I inwardly smiled at the thought of Tom out there fishing, enjoying his freedom in the surf and the wind.

I never saw Nancy or Tom again, but I did receive a phone call from Nancy several years later. Even though they had moved out of state, she had been in touch with a friend here in North Carolina who was experiencing emotional difficulties. Nancy said that she wanted to refer her friend to see me and wondered if I was taking new patients. "But," she said, "before we talk about that, Dr. Day, I want to tell you something." She paused, and then emphatically said, "I'm still healed!"

She updated me on her life: She had never had another panic attack, and her life kept getting better in many ways. She then said again, "I'm healed."

Nancy concluded her update by telling me that she was now in ministry as a speaker for women's conferences and retreats within her denomination. I asked her what she spoke on. She said, "I just tell my life-story, how Perfect Love casts out fear."

In the moment she said that last sentence, I had a shaft of light penetrate my understanding with the wondrous ways of God. He had allowed all those miserable experiences to happen in Nancy's life, experiences in which fear and loneliness seemingly ate up her time and energy. Yet He knew that one day, in His sovereign timing, when

---

[3] Nancy was weaned off her medications under the guidance of her psychiatrist. This is always the safe way to proceed. I believe that sometimes there can be severe physiological imbalances in brain chemistry that require extended use of medication. This was not the case with Nancy.

she turned her heart and her whole life over to Him, chapter by chapter, He would transform and enliven her, and enrich the lives of others through her.

The First Epistle of John 4:18 says, ". . . perfect love casts out fear." That portion of Scripture was no longer just words on a page, it was living in Nancy. She was a witness to that truth, and her life now had a purpose beyond herself—to share this truth with others. She ended her phone call by saying how fulfilling it was to be right in the center of God's purpose for her.

In 1995, at the bottom of her pit of fear, Nancy had desperately prayed for healing. Her prayer had been answered far beyond what she had imagined possible. From the depths of despair to the heights of ministering to women about the power of Love, she was securely in the hands of God like an arrow in the bow and hands of an archer. From the healing that had taken place while in Jesus, the Holy Spirit had launched her into the purposes He had intended for her all along.

Chapter 5

A New Day

In my "training session" with Nancy, the Holy Spirit had shifted me into the role of an assistant and facilitator, but I did not stay in that role for patients who came after Nancy. Rather than directly appealing to the Holy Spirit and trusting His guidance, I would occasionally suggest to patients that God had been with them in the dark, lonely places in their lives . . . and sometimes breakthroughs in healing would occur with this approach.

However, when there was any resistance to my suggestion, or when patients did not see, hear, or sense God's presence, I didn't know what to do next. Slowly I slipped back into my counselor role and continued to dole out advice. I began to read books on "inner healing" and "Spirit-led" ministry, but mostly remained a cognitive Christian counselor, sitting in the driver's seat of therapy sessions.

In my personal life during these years in the 1990s, some healing had begun in me as I absorbed the Word and received counseling. But something vital was missing. My sense of *belonging* was experientially threadbare and I didn't understand why.

In church after church, sermon after sermon, book after book, I heard the repeated message that God was a Father who loved me, forgave me, and now accepted me as His son. But I had the same problem I witnessed in many of my patients, especially the men: I intellectually *knew* of God's love and acceptance in my head, but I didn't really believe or *experience* His love in my heart.

I felt emotionally disconnected and disturbed in my marriage because my wife had wanted to separate and I was now living alone.[4]

---

[4] I don't fault my ex-wife for deciding not to continue in the marriage. During the first decade of being a Christian, my old unstable, dysfunctional self was still firmly in the driver's seat. The Holy Spirit was growing within me but, at best, I considered Him to be a co-pilot.

I also felt detached in my relationship with God. I didn't understand what His perspective was in all this turmoil.

A few years after the conclusion of therapy with Nancy, the parable of the talents kept coming to my attention in sermons and Scripture readings. The end of the parable reads: ". . . And cast the unprofitable servant into the outer darkness. There will be weeping and gnashing of teeth" (Matthew 25:30). Every time I read or heard that passage, I felt a niggling discomfort and would quickly turn my attention elsewhere.

One day, while sitting at my desk, I ran across the parable yet again and felt the same discomfort. This time I spoke inwardly to the Lord: "Lord, please show me the truth about what I am feeling." This time I did not divert my attention away from the emotion. Immediately what emerged out of that murky feeling was a realization, a belief, that *I was that man in the outer darkness.* Then it was no longer a niggling discomfort I felt, it was abject fear.

I stayed with the experience, asking the Holy Spirit to guide me. I inquired why I was in the outer darkness, and a deeper belief came forward into my conscious mind: I believed that *I belonged in the outer darkness because the amount of sin and evil I had done in the 20 years of my wayward, rebellious living was too much to be fully forgiven.*

I was stunned by this revelation and immediately challenged it inwardly with what I had read in the Bible and had learned during the past 12 years: In Jesus I was fully forgiven; He died for all my sins, past, present, and future; His Atonement means I have been reconciled with God and restored to fellowship with Him. However, none of these head-knowledge challenges had any effect on the anxiety and fear in my heart.

In the weeks that followed, I became painfully aware that I could not exchange my inner beliefs with the truths I cognitively knew. It felt like "the wall" between my head and my heart was firmly in place. Through coaching and guidance, I realized two things: (1) these beliefs were deeply entrenched remnants of beliefs from my Catholic upbringing, and (2) my own performance-driven striving would be futile to resolve the issue.

During these weeks, I had memories of my mother telling me to "Be a good boy, Billy," just about every time I left the house as a child. Other memories surfaced, of catechism lessons about God's expectation that I could be good if I tried hard enough—with some help from Him, of course.

The inner turmoil and agitation intensified, and I became increasingly desperate. One day while I was reading the Bible, I discovered these verses in Ezekiel 36:

> I will sprinkle clean water on you, and you will be clean; I will cleanse you from all your impurities and from all your idols. I will give you a new heart and put a new spirit within you; I will remove from you your heart of stone and give you a heart of flesh. And I will put My Spirit in you and move you to follow My decrees and be careful to keep my laws (Ezekiel 36:25-27 NIV).

Upon waking each morning, I prayed through the verses with my heart, soul, mind, and strength. My prayer became a simple, desperate plea: for God to break open my hardened heart and replace it with a heart into which He could and would pour His Spirit.

Breakthrough

This went on for several weeks. Like the persistent friend who comes at midnight (Luke 11:5-9), I kept knocking and asking. I was calling out to God with everything I had. Then one day it happened. I was alone at home, lying prostrate on the floor, crying out to God. I had my Bible with me on the floor. In my mind's eye I saw the word Galatians. I opened the Bible to that epistle and felt inwardly directed to go to Chapter 4, not knowing what I would find there.

I began reading. When my eyes rested on verse 7, "You are no longer a slave but a son," that same personal Presence that had spoken to me in Brightmoor Tabernacle was speaking directly to me again. He was telling me that I was His son. Something in my heart painfully broke, shattered. Next, I felt a softening happen inside . . . and I felt a comforting love flow into my heart. Then a quiet peace.

The lie that I belonged in the outer darkness was blown away by the powerful truth that I was accepted as a son and belonged in the Kingdom. In that moment, I was in God's presence, and I experienced being loved, Father to son. The darkness of fear dissipated.

The relief was incredible. I wept tears of joy. I read the next verse, ". . . and if a son, then an heir of God through Christ," and felt the truth of Jesus saying that He had come to set captives free (Luke 4:18). I felt free, I felt safe, and sensations of coming alive swept into my soul. I belonged. I was on the inside, no longer on the outside. A sense of peace came over me. It was new and it was uncanny, but I eagerly accepted what was happening.

I looked at verse 6, "And because you are sons, God has sent forth the Spirit of His Son into your hearts, crying out, 'Abba, Father!'" I experienced that truth in my heart. It was a new heart, as depicted in those verses of Ezekiel. God had removed my heart of stone and had given me a heart of flesh, into which He was pouring His Spirit.

Over the next weeks, I frequently returned to Galatians 4:7 to hear God whisper those words of truth and love. Tucked away inside of me were more lies and false interpretations of life-experiences that would have to be discovered and swapped out. However, this breakthrough was a beginning.

It now seems as though this event was a replacement "ritual" for the dedication-ritual prayed over me when I was two weeks old. For decades I had lived with a priest-identity, then with no identity at all, mostly feeling isolated and lonely. Now I knew in my head, in my heart, and in my spirit, that I was a beloved son. I belonged.

Building on my aforementioned conversion-experience, this event was a significant deepening of my relationship with God; it was also a powerful therapeutic intervention in the treatment of my anxiety disorder. True heart-healing had begun.

My conversion experience in Brightmoor Tabernacle had for sure felt like dawn after a long night, but this current event felt (and still does) as though it was the first day of my life. It was the day I came to experience that I was a beloved son and that I had a Father to whom I belonged. I was His, and I knew that He had good intentions and purposes for me. He was calling me to participate in His Kingdom. I felt connected and attached at the core of my being, something I had never felt before.

A truth settled into my heart: that the Life of "I am Life" is relational in nature. As a son, in relationship to God my Father, I felt alive. The sense of attachment and belonging was the deepest that I had ever experienced. It was like coming home.

Observations of an Apprentice

The following are observations I noted after the sessions with Nancy (Chapter 4) and after my own powerful healing during this time with God.

1. **The substance of "the wall" which I thought existed between head and heart was actually a lie buried in my mind.** Somehow I had formed a belief which was contrary to the Biblical truth that God has forgiven all my sins in Christ Jesus. I believed that *I had gone over the limit in sinning and couldn't be fully forgiven.* Below the surface of my immediate consciousness, my mind had formed the understanding that my destiny was to be in the outer darkness.

Amazingly, this belief had the power to serve as a deflective shield, turning away thoughts of God's full forgiveness. The lie that *I had not been fully forgiven* was hidden somewhere in the recesses of my mind. Discovering that lie was like finding a secret dungeon in which a part of me was living in darkness, feeling like an outcast. God revealed that lie when I asked Him to show me what was going on.

In a similar way, below the surface of Nancy's immediate consciousness, she had for many years carried around bleak memories of being alone and abandoned at an early age. When God shone the light of His Presence into those memories, the belief that: *I have been abandoned* was replaced by the truth: *God is with me, taking care of me.* This new understanding had a transformative effect on how she saw God, herself, others, and the direction of her life.

As a result of these observations, an interest began to form in me about learning how to access these hidden regions. What was being dismantled in my understanding was the mistaken notion that renewal and healing, as in ". . . be transformed by the renewing of your mind," took place only in the immediate-consciousness part of the human mind. There were more layers to the mind than the *top* layer.

THROUGH ITS MANY LAYERS OF FALSE BELIEFS...

2. Another awareness that broke through was that my full will was not totally available to make whole-hearted decisions. Part of being double-minded *can* be that I have a divided will. Since my profession of faith and full-immersion baptism in 1985, I had been in churches in which it was expected that, with the impartation of the Holy Spirit and the huge body of knowledge in Christian doctrine, a person *should* be transformed in spirit, heart, mind, and behavior. More than once I had heard sermons and counsel about how we *should* "get over it" or "put it behind you," referring to old beliefs and behavior.

Both Nancy and I had stuffed our heads with truths that contradicted the lies we held in our hearts, but these embedded beliefs had been there for years and had formidable override-power. I exerted much effort to *will* God's love down into that place in my heart, but I didn't have 100% of my will available to me. Unbeknown to me, part of my will was locked into the belief *that I was not forgiven*. The Holy Spirit showed me that lie. Then His truth, spoken right into the face of the lie, had the power to break its hold, as I gladly *chose* to receive His truth in place of the lie.

The key insight regarding the will was that the interpretations and conclusions I had come to were not purely cognitive in nature. It was apparent that *belief* was interlaced within these interpretations. I had somewhere, somehow unwittingly chosen to believe that God wouldn't forgive me. When that belief came to the surface, I *released* it and then received God's truth recorded in Galatians 4:7, that *I was His son*. My will became aligned with His will.

3. Finally, in both Nancy and me, healing and transformation happened through the direct intervention of God. He showed up through dialogue and personal involvement, not indirectly through an

application of principles. **It was the personal engagement of God, not human-centered counseling, that accomplished effective healing,**

In Ezekiel 36:25-27, God does *every* action: ~~cleansing, giving a new~~ heart, putting in a new spirit, removing the heart of stone, giving a heart of flesh into which He puts <u>His Spirit, Who then moves the</u> ~~person to keep God's laws.~~ *I THOUGHT EMOTION MOVED US?*

I had experienced the truth of this Scripture: that *God* had done it all by *His* power. My co-laboring consisted of: asking in faith; praying; seeking for truth; being persistent; calling out with everything in me because I was desperate; ceasing from trying or striving to do anything to fix the problem myself; and receiving what the Lord offered. And in Nancy's encounters with the Lord, she had no doubt that, from start to finish, God had cast out her fear with *His* love and had given her *His* peace. For both of us, it was all His doing.

AND ALL OF THAT is FROM AN IGNORANCE OF WHAT REALLY NEEDS TO BE WORKED ON AND AN IGNORANCE OF HOW TO DO IT. BUT GOD!

THE RADICLE INDIFERENCE PLACE RATIONAL.

NO, GAP BETWEEN STIMULAS & RESPONSE is CHRIST/GOD.

EBULIANT!

DOES GOD ONLY ANSWER PRAYER BECAUSE WE ARE CALLING OUT WITH ALL OUR MIGHT AND WE ARE DESPARATE? OR IS IT BECAUSE OUR RIGHTEOUSNESS is SEEN THROUGH CHRIST JESUS. AND WE STAND IN THAT PROMISE BEFORE Him?

Chapter 6

In the Hands of the Potter

From Rejection to Acceptance

Over the next few years, I received much healing from the exchange of truth for distorted beliefs and interpretations of events that had lodged in my soul. Finally the time came for healing the rejection-wound I had carried for decades . . . since the 1960s when I left the seminary. The Holy Spirit brought into the open a buried interpretation I had formed as to why I had to leave. The time was ripe for surgically removing this malignant growth in my soul.

The triggering event which brought to the surface the painful memory is as follows: In the year 2000, I had been invited to join the pastoral staff in the Fellowship of Christ, a church mentioned in Chapter 4. A couple of years later, I had returned home from a retreat in which a discussion about my role in the church had gone awry, mostly because I had been triggered and swamped with thoughts about *being misunderstood*. These thoughts dropped me into feeling isolated and alienated. I was immersed in a swirl of anxiety and extreme discomfort . . . yet I wanted to know the truth about the source of this turmoil. I requested an inner healing session from a colleague.

My ministry facilitator began by having me review and re-experience my emotions and thoughts as they emerged in the discussion with the pastors. Feelings of anger, rejection, and anxiety stood out. Surfacing from these feelings were thoughts of *not measuring up, not belonging,* and *being on the outside.* The feelings and thoughts were much stronger than what might have been generated by the discussion at the retreat, and my facilitator and I prayed to know their origin.

After a few moments, a memory emerged of a time in my late 20s when I was visiting my parents in Minnesota. One night I had mustered the courage to walk into my father's bedroom to ask him a question. The lights were dimmed and he was lying in bed winding down before drifting off to sleep. I had never heard an "I love you" (or anything close to that) from him, and for whatever reason, it was stirred up inside me to ask him what he thought of me. There had been an uncomfortable void in my heart for years and I hoped he might fill it in a satisfying way.

I can't even remember his reply when I asked him what he thought of me because it was so indirect and deflective. I walked out of his bedroom deflated, more empty than before I entered, wishing I had not asked him the question.

The pain from that memory flooded into my awareness in the ministry session, and I prayed for further guidance: What did the Lord want me to know by bringing up this memory? Immediately, in my mind, I was transported into memories of my life in the seminary, strongly experiencing the belief that *I didn't measure up . . . I didn't have the right stuff . . . I didn't make the grade.* Actually, I had been a diligent student, salutatorian and valedictorian of my high school and college graduating classes, respectively, so I was surprised by this last belief about not making the grade.

Then something like a cellar trap door in my mind opened and the beliefs I had buried about why I left the seminary sprang out into the light of full consciousness. The beliefs: *God had decided I didn't have what it took to be in His elite corps of priests. I had been cut from the team. I wasn't good enough. I didn't come up to the grade-level of worthiness to be in the select few He had chosen. He had taken away my vocation to be a priest. God had rejected me.*

Now all the buried pain, anger, and fear spilled out onto the center stage of my mind and heart. Even though the hurt had been stored in my heart for years, when it emerged it had a burning, searing energy as though it were a fresh wound. Sobbing, I held it all up to the Lord and asked Him what He wanted me to know about those beliefs.

Into my mind came large words, MINOR and MAJOR. The first eight years of seminary (high school and college) were called "minor seminary," and the last four years of theology training, following college, were called "major seminary." I saw that for many years I had believed that I wasn't good enough for the *major* seminary, that I was only good enough for the *minor league*, the minor seminary. I believed that I had been cut from the "A" team.

With this revelation, the Holy Spirit then beckoned me to release all of these old beliefs to Him, along with all the pain, as He now poured in thoughts of *His* perspective: *I had not been found unworthy. I had not been cut because I did not have the right stuff. God hadn't rejected me, He had released and liberated me so I could move toward what He had in store for me. He has been grooming and preparing me for such a time as this, right here in North Carolina. The major seminary was not the major league. I am in His major league now because I am in what He has called me to. I measure up because I am in Him and He is equipping me. I may receive and accept that I have been called up to the majors.*

With great relief and tears of joy I allowed the Lord to make the exchange of His truth for the long-held lies. A comforting peace settled into every part of me that had previously been so distraught. I basked in the refreshing waters after so many years of harboring that rejection-belief and the pain it had wrought in me. The "cancer" had been removed and deep healing settled in. I felt immensely relieved and grateful.

Learning to Assist the Master

The decade from 2004-2014 was a time of further healing and training. The field of Christian inner healing was broadening, deepening, and coming more in line with new discoveries, especially in brain science. Previously I have spoken of dealing with lies and wrong interpretations beneath the *top layer of the mind*. Through magnetic resonance imaging (MRI) new light has been shed on the functions of the brain. Turns out it's not top or lower layers as much as *left or right hemispheres*. The left side of the brain is where reasoning, logic, and analysis take place. We store words and explanations here; it is like a storage library. The right brain is non-verbal, imaginative, visual, and knows things by experiencing them.

The emotions and coping strategies of our past experiences are processed in the right brain.

When we are emotionally triggered and overwhelmed by an event in daily life, in order to deal with the current situation, the left brain dims down. Consciousness shifts over to the right-brain remembrance of a previous, *similar* traumatic experience and how a person *interpreted* that traumatic event at the time. Cognitive therapies aimed at changing behavior by coping strategies and conflict-resolution skills are of limited effectiveness because these are all information-concepts stored in the library part (left hemisphere) of the brain. Interpretations, beliefs, and emotions are all woven into the experiences processed in the right brain—the area that must be accessed in order to facilitate effective change.

Let me tell a story as an illustration of this process. A 40 year-old man is always frightened by any encounter with dogs. At age five he had innocently approached a dog to pet him and the dog bit him. In processing this event at the time, a belief was formed as part of the experiential recording in his right brain: *Dogs are vicious animals and will hurt me.*

From that point on, the boy is frightened of dogs and this continues into his adult years. He reads about dogs to gain mastery over his fear and even goes into counseling for the issue. One day he is returning home from a therapy session in which the counselor has once again reinforced his left-brain storage tank with positive thoughts that most dogs are not vicious and most often there is nothing to be afraid of. "Be wary but calm," the counselor says.

The man leaves the therapy session feeling calm and reassured, thinking he is making progress in overcoming his fear. He walks around the corner of a building and encounters a woman who is out walking a small dog on a leash. The man immediately shifts into fear and his heart starts racing. He recoils and is ready to run.

What has happened is that, in a flash, the sight of the dog has triggered his unresolved trauma from childhood. All the fear from his traumatic event at age five comes roaring to the surface. His left-brain rational information has little power to deal with the situation because his left brain has gone offline.

In my counseling practice during the years after 2000, it seemed more and more futile to be shuffling around thoughts in the cognition-storehouse of the left brain or tinkering with behavior that was really coming from internal, negative beliefs from the brain's experiential knowledge-base. By 2008, for those patients who were ready and could receive it, I functioned as a surgical assistant to the Master Surgeon who removed soul-growths of lies and wrongful interpretations of events. He then filled those places in the soul with His love, truth, assurance, and peace.

Perhaps my family of origin was given a glimpse of God's purposes for me and formed the only interpretation that made sense to them within their culture of Roman Catholicism. I don't know, but I have accepted it all—from conception to the present—as the unfolding of God's plan. He is The Potter, I am the clay. As I let the clay rest in His hands, He shapes it into a vessel of His design and intention.

God continues to mold and shape whatever I give Him. I have been a small-town boy from Minnesota, a Catholic seminarian, a university theology instructor, a humanistic social worker, a transpersonal psychologist, a Christian counselor, a pastor of counseling and inner healing ministry . . . and now a hybrid psychotherapist/minister/coach. And, foremost, I am a husband, father, grandfather, and friend. I give all of this to the Lord, for Him to use as He will in accomplishing His purposes, because I know and have experienced that *my real identity is being His son*.

Transitioning to Part II of the Story

The questions I explore in PART II are fundamental questions pertaining to all areas of life—individual, family, community. The word *transformation* has become popular in the fields of both psychological and spiritual counseling, to express *significant change*. "Trans-formation" has come to mean anything from superficial modification to radical renewal. But what is real transformation? What *degree of change* is necessary to bring about real healing, wholeness, and fulfillment in these areas of life that are so muddled, snarled, and corrupted in seemingly incorrigible ways?

In Part II, I will share conclusions that I have pulled together in answering these questions. Then I will describe how these conclusions are supported in Scripture and experience. Finally, I will demonstrate the dynamics of transformation in daily life.

PART II

The Dynamics of Transformation

Chapter 7

Gathering the Threads

First Thread: The Indoctrination Illusion

The worldview in which I lived for my first 21 years had much more to do with indoctrination than transformation. As a baptized Roman Catholic, I was told that I had been given a salvation-ticket to heaven, and it was my job to stay out of sin so I could keep my ticket and arrive safely at my destination.

Much of my education in elementary school and in the seminary was information about how to offset attacks against safe passage to heaven. According to Church doctrine, I could lose my salvation-ticket to heaven by having unconfessed mortal sins on my soul.

I was taught that Jesus died for my sins and rose from the dead to make a way for me to go to heaven, but there was sparse teaching about a personal God who wanted to change me *now*. The whole program poured into my brain was about making it to heaven by prayer, receiving the sacraments, and staying focused on avoiding sin through sheer willpower. A need for the *radical change* implicit in the word *transformation* was diluted by the Catholic doctrine of "grace builds on nature."

This doctrine meant that human nature supposedly retained its basic integrity, however impaired it might have become by the continuous corrosion of sin. Grace was the divine help needed to stay clean and holy by correct thoughts and behavior. The image that comes to mind is a house that is maintained by regular cleaning and maintenance repairs—things like leaky faucets and broken tiles. But the basic foundation, structural beams, and roof are assumed to be intact and functional.

In the more progressive theology of Marquette University, our original human nature was still viewed as having basic, functional integrity. God's love was seen as a force to upgrade one's old nature, but there was no sense that *radical* change was needed.

It was not until years later that I saw the true state of my "house": the black mold on the inside of the drywall, the rotting wooden beams, the deep cracks and fissures in the foundation, and the barely visible holes in the roof through which outside elements silently seeped in to gradually yet inexorably corrode the entire interior of the house. The truth was that my house needed a *total makeover!*

Strangely absent in all this education was the teaching of Jesus that humans need to be born again, or born from above (John 3:3), a regeneration He coupled with the importance of believing fully *into* Him (John 3:16). Not taking this directive seriously seems amazing to me now, because right there in the Gospel of John is the clear, basic principle and process of transformation: **to start life in a totally new way by immersion into Jesus so that His Spirit can fashion me anew.** There is also the vivid analogy that Jesus gave in Matthew 9:17 about putting new wine into new wineskins, not into patched up old ones.

Second Thread: The Information Fantasy

Around age 25, I made my escape from Catholicism during the two years I taught liberal theology at the Universities of Portland and Santa Clara. Catholicism had become confining to the breaking point, and I broke loose (at least intellectually) by classroom rants against the futility of legalistic doctrines and performance-based behavior modification. My lectures focused on how much God loved us, but it was still just talk *about* God, without engaging directly *with* Him.

Leaving Catholicism behind and accepting a broader (liberal Protestant) understanding of Christianity was not difficult because it felt as though I was escaping a prison. However, the "fresh air" of the ideas (information) about institutional Christianity being dead and outdated was short-lived.

As I said in Chapter 2, Jesus had been experienced as a dogma-Jesus and a ritual-Jesus, not a living person with whom I genuinely interacted. Changing ideas about Jesus seemed refreshing for a while, but without a personal and living relationship, the entire edifice was on shaky ground. By the time I arrived in San Diego to obtain a Master's degree in Social Work, the ideas *about* God and even the idea *of* God were fading fast.

I was neither free nor happy during my 25 years of supposedly living a "Christian" life. Mostly I felt anxious, frustrated, and restless— and ready to jump into life in a new way. In San Diego I did not have concrete thoughts about needing transformation, though I intuitively knew that something needed to change because I felt so deadened inside.

However, I was still attached to pursuing new information as the way to find the *life* my soul so deeply desired. I loaded up on more information in San Diego (Humanism), and tried to apply it in Napa. Like the other information-systems I had pursued in searching for truth, this one also crashed and burned.

Traveling abroad was an attempt to shed all the information about life that had proved to be useless. But I loaded up the New Age worldview, thinking it was the magic thought-system that would be the answer.

When the New Age light dimmed and I re-entered Christianity through my experience in Brightmoor Tabernacle, and in the subsequent healing I described in Chapters 3-6, I at first reverted to my pattern of downloading a new worldview, a new source of information. However, I encountered something much more substantial and life-changing than a new batch of ideas. I didn't re-enter Christianity as a religious system; *I was drawn into a relationship with Jesus in which actual transformation took place*, for the first time in my life.

- From these first two threads, I have a conclusion to share:[5] <u>Indoctrination and Information do not generate trans-formation.</u> Some change and adaptation can occur by these means, but not the radical change necessary to produce real healing and lasting peace.

---

[5] A reminder that these conclusions are formed from my experiences and from my understanding of Scripture.

For now, I will simply let this statement stand as a kind of experiential principle that has become apparent after all my years of searching. What I mean by this first conclusion will become clearer as the Biblical basis of transformation unfolds in upcoming chapters.

Third Thread: The Self-Sufficiency Delusion

The delusion of self-sufficiency has been discovered mostly through my experiences within Humanism and New Age spirituality.

Humanism. San Diego and Napa were experiments in pulling the plug and letting drain out any belief in God. I saturated my mind with many variations of the Human Potential Movement in psychology, absorbing and applying the theory that mankind has within themselves the self-sufficient power for success in realizing all their dreams. At first I was excited by what I thought was the liberating answer to overcoming and settling the internal chaos of my soul, as well as the answer to societal problems. That giddiness was short-lived.

In Chapter 2, I said that "Napa hit me smack in the face." The *information* I had absorbed in San Diego was totally inadequate in the face of the complex psychological and social problems I encountered as a social worker. And this same information provided a woefully impotent response to the emotional turmoil that roared through my soul. The experiment of Humanism died there in Napa; I found its promise to be disturbingly untrue.

However, another variation of "everything I need is totally within me" was waiting in the wings, and this variation presented itself as the sweet celestial elixir that would satisfy my soul.

New Age Spirituality. In New Age spirituality, a promise was extended that there was a way of finding real self, of finding truth, of becoming more loving. This "promised land" of *enlightenment* could supposedly be discovered within a journey through meditation, advanced esoteric knowledge, secret skills, artistic expression, and spiritual healing. I never found this promised land, though I spent 14 years seriously pursuing it.

In reflecting on these 14 years, now that I have moved on, I see that this phase of my life could be called *self-deification*. In New Age spirituality, I practiced meditation techniques and consulted New Age psychologists in my endeavors to transcend my separate-self and move into the divine expanse of "Higher Self." God was viewed as an impersonal, Star Wars-type Force that flows through everything and everyone. In this understanding, there is no holy, personal God who holds standards, purpose, or design. There is no one to offend or disrespect. There is no one to be accountable to—except *me*, "Divine" me.

However, the truth was that, far from becoming enlightened and loving, I turned more inward and introspective than ever before. Egocentricity subtly grew by leaps and bounds. My carefully cultivated sense of entitlement was placed on its highest throne yet. And arrogance and pride rose to new levels of grandiosity.

As a result of all these endeavors I did not evolve, transform, or change . . . except that I burrowed more deeply into myself. If anything, I became more arrogant, prideful, and deluded than ever before. I was totally lost and am truly grateful for the divine intervention that began in the sanctuary of Brightmoor Tabernacle in 1984.

The revelation that the attachments I had cultivated during those 14 years were artificial life-supports and not real life was sobering and life-changing. Going deeper, in the years after 1984, the discovery of the depth of my self-absorption and its resultant moral depravity (Chapter 3), served to tear off the celestial mask of the New Age garment I had tried on for truth-fit. When I was willing to look below the surface of my self-centeredness, what I experienced shattered the mirage of New Age spirituality.

Having this mask torn off was a turning point in my life, and I began to walk the first two steps as articulated in *The Big Book* of Alcoholics Anonymous: "We admitted we were powerless . . . . Came to believe that a Power greater than ourselves could restore us to sanity." What I was shown below the surface-waters of my soul was a pervasive, depraved, addictive attachment to myself, and I was helpless and powerless to break free of this addiction by my own resources. In truth, I was not free.

As this delusional veil of self-sufficiency dropped, a truth shone forth brightly and has been a daystar ever since: *I was impossibly entangled and needed someone to rescue me. I needed a Rescuer who had the power to free me.*

Jesus' words on the subject illumine and match my experience. In Luke 4:18-21, Jesus says that He has been sent "to set captives free." In John 8:34 Jesus says that those who sin habitually are "enslaved." Then He says, "Now a slave has no permanent place in the family, but a son belongs to it forever. So if the Son sets you free, you will be free indeed" (vv. 35-36). And the New Testament is full of references to being enslaved and then set free by Jesus.

In the powerful inner healing session I described in Chapter 5, I was invited to receive these words: "Therefore you are no longer a slave but a son, and if a son then an heir of God through Christ" (Galatians 4:7). As I write these words today, 20 years later, I experience what I am expressing here. I have truly been set free and it is a wondrous, joyful state. The details of this freedom will emerge in the remainder of the book, but I wanted to tell you this much right away.

- From this third thread, another conclusion to share: <u>Self-sufficiency is a delusion.</u>

Fourth Thread: The Transforming Power of Person-to-Person Interactions

In Catholicism, God seemed like a remote overseer who constantly evaluated and critiqued performance. From an early age, I felt that He was more likely to focus on what I had done wrong than on anything else. Later, my belief that God had cut me from the elite squad of priest-trainees reinforced this image and kept me at arms' length from Him for many years. That image is in sharp contrast to now knowing my Father, the Lord Jesus, and the Holy Spirit as three

Persons who together love me dearly and are unreservedly poised to bring about the best for me in any given moment of my life.

When God made His presence known on that day back in 1984, when He said "I am Life," I had an unfamiliar sense of an awesome Presence that was coming from beyond . . . yet I also had a familiar sense of here-and-now personal dialogue. There was a *person* speaking the words, a person who was somehow clearly *other* than me, yet was not remote. This person was warm and inviting, yet firm and clear in the unambiguous nature of the exchange He offered: Himself as my life-source in place of my current life-support attachments.

As the years have passed since that moment, and as I have had more encounters and dialogues with God, I have become deeply convinced that this trinity-of-Persons God does His best and most powerful work in the giving-and-receiving dynamic of personal relationships.

He doesn't distribute a *part* of Himself, as the description of *grace* so often connotes—as though God deposits a divine substance into our souls as a man might drop money into the hands of a homeless person on the street. In the many inner healing sessions I have received and facilitated, over and over again God shows up as a Person who radiates Truth, Love, and Life from the core of His Being to the core of my being. As Psalm 42:7 puts it: "Deep calls to deep."

I have found that when I or my patients receive *Truth*—not as reading information, but as Jesus speaking truth within the unresolved experiences of life—transformative change occurs. When I listen and hear Jesus say that I am no longer a slave but a son, or when a patient hears Jesus tell her that she is a winner not a loser, seismic shifts occur in the minds and hearts of recipients.

Jesus said that He *is* Truth. I have discovered that this doesn't mean He dispenses a storehouse of principles and concepts, like handing folks an operations manual and telling them to read it. When Jesus speaks truth, He radiates the very reality and power of truth through His words, His character, and His heart. He doesn't just dispense truth; He, as a Person, *is* Truth.

STONE PLATES BENEATH THE SURFACE SHIFTS

For example, I once told a patient that her sexual abuse at age four was not her fault. My words were helpful and soothing but they did not have the power to swap out her false and oppressive sense of shame and guilt. In a later session, however, within the presence and leading of the Spirit of Jesus Christ, Jesus said to her, "It wasn't your fault." *His* personal power crushed and disposed of the lie that had been embedded in her soul for 40 years. Truth, expressed in the Person of Jesus, set her free (John 8:32).

Further, she experienced *identity-alteration*. Her shame-shackles were broken (and stayed broken), and she felt free to be *a beloved child of God* for the first time in her life. The verse of Romans 12:2 came alive for her in the vivid glow of realized and internalized truth: ". . . be transformed by the renewing of your mind, that you may prove what is that good and acceptable and perfect will of God."

The context of personal relationship is the medium through which the transaction of exchange takes place. God is *Love*. When His love is received by a person who acknowledges Him as a person and speaks with Him as such, God's awesome power is present *within* the relationship.

For example, in Chapter 4, when my patient Nancy opened her faith to believe that God had been with her in that dark bedroom when she was a young girl, He let her know that He had been there all along, in the person of Jesus loving her. The sense of Jesus' personal loving presence was the context within which transformation took place. She internalized a new identity as a beloved daughter of God. During the months I knew Nancy, I watched Love Itself cast out her fear (1 John 4:18). I watched God create her anew, Person to person.

Being loved and loving are realities that point to a core component of real change and transformation. I know and value the healing and nurturing that occur when humans love one another. But I believe there is a *God-shaped void in every human heart* that only He can fill. Part of the freedom I now have is knowing Whose I am (realizing that I belong in God's family) and experiencing that God's love completes me and makes me whole, in a way that no human love can.

I had been loved well by several persons in my life before I received God's personal love for me. However, during those years I felt restless, insecure, and incomplete. God's love alone has yielded by far the most powerful and permeating transformation in my life, bringing about not only a sense of *finding* myself but also of *knowing who I am*—which feels more like the beginning of an adventure than the end of a hunt.

My relationship with God is the *foundational* place within which my life is re-aligned in transformative ways. God definitely can, and does, weave His will and His ways through a variety of loving human relationships here on earth; but however healing and nurturing my human relationships are, they are *supplemental*, not foundational.

I have not yet mentioned that I married again, in 2003. Our marriage is an example of what I mean by the difference between foundational and supplemental. Before we met, both my wife, Susan, and I had finally allowed God to fill the God-shaped space in each of our hearts. We both knew who we were in Him and had individually received significant transformative healing from Him.

On November 15, 2003, in our exchange of wedding vows, we promised to help one another stay faithful to the *first love* of our lives, the Lord Jesus. Then we exchanged our vows to one another in what we called our *second love*. We have been married for 14 years and continue to grow in love, experiencing the mutual healing, comfort, and companionship that exist within the giving and receiving of our relationship. However, for us, the relationship that each of us has with God is the wellspring and source of <u>*Life*</u> from which our love for one another flows and is sustained.

- A third and final conclusion: <u>God alone, Person to person, transforms lives.</u>

Such are the threads and preliminary conclusions I have gathered together from the course of my life. They will be expanded upon in the chapters that follow by descriptions of the nature and process of transformation, as per Scripture and experience.

To start with, in my third conclusion above, I assert that God transforms within a person-to-person relationship. Is it Scriptural, is it possible, and is it real to talk about interacting with God in such a personal way? Chapter 8 is an exploration of this three-pronged question.

Chapter 8

Interacting with God

For the first 42 years of my life, any activity involving God was one-sided. I did all the talking and wasn't interested in or trained to listen. In childhood and into adult years, I talked to God by asking for things, telling Him how majestic He was, asking for help, requesting protection from the wiles of the devil, and confessing sins. Throughout my Catholic years, I had a sense of living in two separate worlds—a *religious* world of prayer, Mass, and sacraments, and a *daily-life* world. God was in charge of the first world, I was in charge of the second, though I believed I needed His help to get through. As a seminarian and a theologian, there was a third world: a *mental* world filled with thoughts and doctrines about God.

In all three worlds, God-talk was plentiful but God Himself seemed removed and remote. I didn't have any idea that I could just talk with Him as though God was a person standing next to me. Even the thought of the Holy Spirit being within me seemed abstract and impersonal. The mutuality implied in the word *interaction* was missing.

Absent in all those years was a simple, conversational context in which I might ask a question like, "Lord, what is your perspective on this situation?" —with an expectation that He would answer, and that I could listen and directly receive His answer.

After my years in Humanism, and as I slipped into a New-Age spiritual mindset, God became an impersonal Force that I believed could be felt or intuited in the right circumstances. Names such as *Universal Consciousness*, *The Source*, or *The Universe* were used to describe God, but such abstract concepts ruled out personal engagement.

Phrases such as "I thank the Universe" or "I think the Universe is telling me to change careers" were typical expressions I heard and repeated, but there was no personal dimension in which to have dialogue or interaction. Similar to my Catholic days, it never dawned on me that personal engagement with God was possible.

In 1984, at age 42, God initiated interaction by speaking "I am Life," and I responded by pulling the plug on my many pseudo life-supports. Several years later, I sat at a kitchen table, a Bible open in front of me, and directly asked God to show me whether or not this book was His inspired Word.

As I read some passages, the words came alive. Someone alive was speaking the verses. My question was being answered personally. This marked the beginning of conversational prayer with God. However, more years would go by before a flow of conversation became normal and regular.

In the first years following the year 2000, the process of Jesus-centered inner healing (sometimes called *listening prayer*) opened up new dimensions in experiencing how much God desires to engage with us personally. All of the healing sessions in which I participated during these early years after 2000 took place within the context of dialogues with Him. His personal presence becomes more and more real as I have continued to facilitate inner healing sessions through engaging directly with the Lord.

Playing Above the Rim

As I write about how I gradually moved into a two-way relationship with God, an analogy keeps coming to mind that illustrates the shift away from a one-way "relationship." Time for a sports story.

I played varsity basketball in high school and college during the years 1956-1964. At 6'3" I played the position of forward in high school, but in college we had a taller team and I played the guard position. Not long ago I was touring a sports museum with my brother, Pat, and I stopped in the basketball area to watch some old video clips of professional basketball games. It was 1954. There was the legendary George Mikan, 6'10", playing center for the Minneapolis Lakers. The ball is thrown to him, wide open, near the basket. He jumps up, arms slightly bent at the elbows as he holds the ball with both hands . . . then gives the ball a little push-shot into the basket from his fingers, which are about two inches below the rim. I was amazed, he did not dunk it. I watched more of the game and saw several players, all 6'5'' or taller, make moves to the basket without dunking . . . apparently without even the *thought* of dunking the ball through the hoop. Then I realized, it was the 1950s and no one dunked. Many players could have dunked; they had the height and the athletic ability. But at 10 feet, the rim was the ceiling, not actually but in the *minds* of the players, coaches, and spectators.

As I watched the video, I remembered playing in a college basketball game with Bill Menzel, the center on our team. He was about 6'8". Like George Mikan, he would go up with the ball and pop it into the basket, his fingers near the rim. In my memory there was a vague sense of something being not quite right with that shot, but my own mindset at that time, like a mental cataract, did not let the "obvious" thought through: "Bill, you're tall enough and have adequate jumping ability . . . just jam the ball through the hoop!" It was not until somewhere in the 1960s that the mental barrier, like a glass ceiling, was shattered. And then, with the regular visuals on TV of NBA star, Julius Irving, routinely dunking the ball, the whole game of basketball began to be played *above the rim*.

As I was writing this chapter, the story above has played through my mind several times. For 42 years I played *below the rim* in my relationship with God. In 1984, in a sovereign manner, He crashed through the glass ceiling of my mindset when He spoke to me in a church setting. But the webbing of that mindset was thick. It took several years and many incursions "above the rim" (His speaking and my daring to jump into His Presence to inquire of Him and receive from Him) before the restricted understanding of what is possible would finally be broken apart. I now know that the invitation to "come boldly to the throne . . ." (Hebrews 4:16) is an invitation to come into direct dialogue with the Lord Himself.

So how could a one-way relationship (I do all the talking) have taken hold of my thinking for so long, to the extent that I hadn't a single thought that personal dialogue was possible?

There is a prevailing mindset in many churches, including the one I grew up in, that believes God spoke through the writers of the Bible and then stopped speaking. This thinking views the Word of God as totally contained and captured in the pages of a book. It is similar to the doctrine of the Sadducees in Jesus' time, which taught that God stopped speaking after He finished speaking with Moses.

Let me be clear, I believe that the Bible is the written Word of God. It is a written record of the saving truth spoken by God, and reliably sets the boundaries and parameters of what He has to say to humankind. But the Word of God is not just the Bible. The Bible is not Jesus Christ who is the living Word of God. Jesus Himself said to these Sadducees, "You search the Scriptures because you think that in them you have eternal life; it is these that bear witness of Me; and you are unwilling to come to Me so that you may have life" (John 5:39-40). The Bible points to Jesus, the fount of life.

The wooden thinking that views the Word of God as totally *contained* inside the pages of a book cannot conceive of the spiritual reality of God *continuing to speak*. For many of my 42 years, I embraced this wooden thinking. Now I know for myself that God does not intend the Bible to be a static receptacle, a repository to be intellectually accessed and then stored in my mind, like a reference book in a library.

I have thought of the Bible in this way, as though it were a user's manual for a car . . . to learn the way God wants my life to operate, then to apply the directions I find in the manual. But now I know that God speaks to me, Person to person, through the power of the Holy Spirit. When I read Scripture, I first anchor myself by prayer into the presence of the Holy Spirit. I become aware of my relationship with the Lord, and I begin to listen to Him and wait on Him to speak to me on this day, in this moment, as I enter into dialogue with Him.

Sometimes He speaks to me through the written words of the Bible, and sometimes He speaks to me in words that are not direct quotes from the Bible but are in accord with the written Word. His is a *living* Word, not just because it is lively, meaningful, and rich in content. His Word is a living Word because *He is still speaking*. It is not a past tense, done deal. He wants to continue speaking with whomever will listen, and I have finally begun to listen.

When Jesus made a personal connection with my patient, Nancy, via an image of Himself and words of love, the Word of God was still speaking. Perfect Love was casting out fear (1 John 4:18). When Jesus told me I was no longer a slave but a son, God was still speaking the words of Galatians 4:7 to me in the present moment.

There is still a lot of religious fog hiding the relational reality of God and hiding the continuous acts of God in any moment. I believe the following: He is still breathing His Life into us, making us living souls (Genesis 2:7); we live and move and have our being in Him (Acts 17:28); He speaks through the marvelous natural world of His creation; He speaks through images, pictures, and parables; He speaks in the circumstances of our lives; He speaks directly to us in conversation; and He speaks as we worship Him individually and corporately. He has never stopped speaking His reality since the beginning: "In the beginning was the Word . . ." (John 1:1). The question is, *will we listen and respond?*

From my experiences of the past 30 years, something wells up inside of me that would like to blast away this short-sighted mental cataract—an obstruction that functions much like the pre-1960's restrictive thought of the basketball rim being the ceiling. Scripturally and experientially, I know that God "plays" in the "game" of life way above the rim. I believe He would have us stretch up in faith to meet Him, to interact with Him. He wants to talk with us in two-way conversations. I feel His eagerness to do so. [6]

Dangerous Waters

Yes, the potential for danger lurks in encouraging people to hear from God and to experience His presence. People can go off the deep

---

[6] For anyone who wants guidance for conversing with God, I recommend David Takle: **kingdomformation.org**, and Mark Virkler: **cwgministries.org**. On their websites you will find Biblical documentation and practical guidelines for a conversational relationship with God.

end. "Voices" can be one's own inner self-talk, auditory and visual hallucinations from pathologically disturbed minds, or demonic voices that come to us through ungodly thoughts and perceptions.

As whole denominations and churches have plunged into mysticism and wildly charismatic streams, a shudder runs through us when we hear the words, "God told me." Abject foolishness and devastating tragedy have followed in the wake of those words—witness the utterances of defunct American cult leaders, Jim Jones and David Koresh. There are counterfeits, fakery, and confusion. Keen discernment is needed now more than ever.

However, there is another danger: going off the *shallow* end. This is a more "respectable" danger, but as devastating and distorting as the deep end. One day Jesus walked into a synagogue and healed a blind man on the Sabbath. The Jewish leaders, proud of being Moses' disciples, "knew" that Jesus could not possibly be God because working on the Sabbath was clearly not allowed. They "knew" the Scriptures, and Jesus was clearly a sinner.

Even when confronted by the healed blind man, who said "One thing I do know, that though I was blind, now I see" (John 9:25), the Pharisees rejected the work because it did not conform to their legalistic ideas. They said, "We know that God has spoken to Moses, but as for this man, we do not know where He comes from" (v. 29).They did not know the living God in His Love and Mercy, even though He was standing there in front of them.

With the same legalistic fervor, many denominations react to "charismania" (extreme variations of the Charismatic Movement) by shutting down the possibility of hearing from God and experiencing Him in personal interactions. Of course we must be wary, but there is no Scriptural evidence for the total denial of hearing from God. Quite the contrary.

Examples abound in Scripture of "playing above the rim," that is, personally interacting with the Lord.

In the Old Testament, (1) There is the amazing passage in 1 Samuel 3:9-10 in which Samuel says, "Speak, Lord, for your servant is listening." And after this passage, Samuel's life of having two-way conversations with God unfolds. (2) Moses dialogued with God as two friends might talk (Exodus 33:11, for example).

In the New Testament, (3) Jesus often spoke about listening prayer, and daily devoted time to converse with His Father. The conversations were not one-way prayer speeches; He was in dialogue with His Father: ". . . for all things that I have heard from My Father I have made known to you" (John 15:15). And then He prays in John 17:3 "that they may know You, the only true God, and Jesus Christ whom You have sent." It is a prayer towards having the same interaction with the Father that He has. Also, in John 16:13-15, Jesus tells us clearly that the Holy Spirit will be coming and "will guide you into all truth," and that "whatever He hears He will speak . . . . He will take of Mine and declare it to you." (4) In Paul's conversations with the Lord, three times he begged Him to remove the famous "thorn in the flesh." God was not silent. He responded and said, "My grace is sufficient for you, for My strength is made perfect in weakness" (2 Corinthians 12:9). How did God speak to Paul: In an audible voice? By the "still small voice" (1 Kings 19:12)? Or did God join His thought to Paul's receptive thinking, and the two thoughts became one in Paul's mind? I don't know, but whatever the case, Paul directly pleaded before the Lord, and the Lord responded.

Interacting with God and the Process of Transformation

Back in 1984, in Brightmoor Tabernacle, when I heard the words "I am life," I felt hope, but I was wary. As far as I knew, this was the next adventure of my ongoing explorations looking for truth and healing. I decided to immerse myself in the experience, but my intention was to discover whether or not this "life" was real and to know whether or not the person who spoke was real.

The remaining paragraphs of this section are reflections that answer the questions of whether or not I have found this Person to be real and whether or not what He has to offer is real. Have I found truth? Have I found healing? Have I found *life*?

The title of Chapter 5 is *A New Day*. I mean the word "Day" to refer to my last name as well as to indicate a sense of newness that came upon me when the Lord spoke the words, "You are no longer a slave but a son." In a way, it feels like that was the first day of my life. The chasm of separation from my decades-long detachment disorder was filled in with the substance of *belonging, relational attachment,* and *identity.* Since that day, the chasm is no more. Similar to the centurion's servant in Matthew 8:9, Jesus spoke the word and I was healed.

For many years I had pursued people, knowledge, drugs, and therapies of many varieties. However, the separation-pain had always remained and the varieties of "reality" I found had always proved to be illusory. I can't adequately describe the healing that has settled into my soul through the sense of *belonging in my true family of origin in the kingdom of God*; but I can tell you that it feels transformative, of caterpillar-to-butterfly proportions.

In Chapter 6, I recounted the inner healing experience I received in which the deeply buried cancerous lie that *God had rejected me* was expunged from my soul with one swift stroke from the Surgeon's scalpel. The truth of God's love and purposes for me poured in to close the wound and replace a sense of *rejection* with an awesome, overwhelming balm of *acceptance.*

Over the previous decades, I had gone to extreme measures to deal with this rejection wound. Nothing worked. It is now almost 14 years since the time of that healing. I can say the words in the Book of Zephaniah 3:17, *that the Lord has calmed and quieted me with His love.* As I write, I feel His love. I feel peace.

So, the results of my decision in 1984 to plunge into "life" have been remarkably effective, life-changing, and transforming. I have discovered truth, I have found healing, and I am immersed in a relationship that is Real.

A Final Note on Playing Above the Rim

This chapter is very significant in the story I am narrating because my transformative changes and healings have all taken place within interactions with the Lord. When I willingly let myself be drawn into Him, He introduced me to His above-the-rim dimension of personal engagement. In that interpersonal realm, He has done amazing "dunks" of healing and life-changes.

I feel as though I am now plunged into a grand adventure. I know it is likely to be a wild ride at times, but I have looked into the eyes of Jesus and I know that He is good.

The words of Psalm 34:8 are experientially true for me: "Taste and see that the Lord is good." More and more I feel encouraged to trust Him with my life. It seems that this is what happens when you continue to play above the rim. It's scary, but liberating too. As Jesus told us in John 8:36, "If the Son makes you free, you shall be free indeed."

Chapter 9

Transformation and Identity

Self-Image and God-Image

After working in the field of psychotherapy for the past 40 years, I am convinced that we tend to live out the mental images of ourselves that are formed during our early developmental years. These are *self-images*. Also formed there are pictures of God: *God-images*. We position ourselves in relationship to God according to these images. I have seen this phenomenon on display in many of my patients, as well as in myself.

Growing up, I internalized a self-image of having the special destiny of being a priest. Part of this inner formation was a sense of belonging to an elite corps. It was a sense of being drafted (military style) from birth to serve as one of God's chosen few to help lead His flock. Ego-inflating pride and a sense of superiority poured into this self-image. Slowly but surely I became encased in egocentricity.

When I felt as though my precious jewel of a vocation to be a priest had been removed, I buried the inner interpretation, that *I was not good enough for God's elite corps of priests,* into the murky depths of denial. I didn't really have a relationship with God, I had a relationship with a sense of worth based on being chosen to be a priest. Internalizing the belief that I had been un-chosen (rejected), caused my sense of worth to plummet.

The God-image formed in me from an early age was a no-nonsense cop and judge who could come down hard on transgressors (even if you were one of the chosen few). Having an emotionally distant father reinforced the sense of distance between God and me. In addition, my understanding of my relationship with God was heavily performance-based. If I did not perform well in life, I could lose God's love and favor.

I didn't know specifically why I had been found unworthy to continue in the seminary, but my quick decision to become a lay theologian was no doubt whistling in the dark abyss of unworthiness. Nothing was left when the entire basis for my sense of worth was pulled out from under me. Upon leaving the seminary, a cavernous sinkhole indeed opened up inside of me.

By the time I dove into Humanism in Graduate School in San Diego, I had stopped trying to earn God's love back by being a good lay theologian. The religion of Christianity had run its course and I turned to the Human Potential Movement. I put my human self squarely on the throne for three years, but this solution collapsed quickly in Napa. Humanism was like printing my own money for three years and then discovering the money was counterfeit.

The foray into New Age spirituality was a similar printing-my-own-money venture, but I didn't recognize it as such for many years. I was drawn to the positive self-esteem, coupled with a new God-image, i.e., a Force rather than a Person to whom I was accountable. It was a seemingly good solution for a while. My early self-image of entitlement and grandiosity flourished, and believing that I was inherently one with Universal Consciousness (God) nicely covered up the buried belief of unworthiness.

In 1984, after my experience in Brightmoor Tabernacle, a seismic shift began that has shaken me to the core of my being. I believe that this shaking has been the Holy Spirit moving through my soul once I said that I wanted to enter into a relationship with the Person who said "I am Life." Part of the shaking has been an obliteration of various self-images and God-images that I had held in my mind and acted out in my daily life.

The Holy Spirit began breaking up old God-images as I engaged with the Word of God in a new way, and as I engaged with a personal God who loved me. But there was the hardened core of encased egocentricity that had to be addressed. It was definitely a God-sized problem to break through and resolve by *His* solution, not a solution of my making.

In the years following 1984, when I was finally willing to get real and look soberly at what was inside my soul, I saw what was truly there. Yes, there was some good stuff, but there was also a hidden heart that had become hardened by substantial strata of a judgmental, resentful, lustful, easily offended, self-absorbed mindset. It was an entrenched mindset and, when exposed and acknowledged, the need for God's intervention was as clear as day.

In Chapter 5, I recounted the story of how God broke into my hardened heart in a stone-shattering way, revealing to me that I was no longer enslaved to my old self but free because I was now grafted into Him as a son. The difficult dynamic to express here is the *exchange* that happened at the level of *identity*. God's revelation, together with my heart-felt acceptance of being His son, dissolved my lifelong self-image of being isolated, of being a solo-unit unto myself. I now *belonged* somewhere. My sense of self expanded from being solitary to being a family member. And my lifelong God-image of a distant, cop-like God also shifted dramatically. I have experienced His love and closeness more and more since that day.

The intervention of God telling me who I am and demonstrating at the same time who He is has constituted a core component of my transformation. This shift in identity was administered by God, Person to person, and it was a change that only God could accomplish. Many times I had tried to change my self-image . . . like the old adage of trying to pull yourself up by yanking on your own boot straps. My experience is that identity-change is a big thing, and it is a God thing.

Self-Image, God-Image, and Lies

Discovering buried lies is an important part in this process because much of the formation of self-images and God-images is hidden from conscious view, having been developed in earlier years. Such was the case when The Holy Spirit surfaced a hidden belief that *I belonged in the outer darkness because the amount of sin and evil I had done was too much to be forgiven.* When I chose to release that malignant belief, the way was cleared to receive the self-image that God wanted me to have in my mind and heart. Such was also the case with a patient who came to me several years ago.

Alex had just lost his wife through divorce and was about to lose his third career. He was desperate to know why he kept sabotaging every endeavor in his life. As we prayed for the Holy Spirit to show him the answer to his desperate plea, a long-forgotten memory surfaced.

In the memory, he was at his high school's state wrestling tournament, in a match against the reigning champion in his weight class. He had become an excellent wrestler by staying long hours after school to practice so he wouldn't have to return home to his critical father, who repeatedly yelled at him that *he would never amount to anything and he was a loser.* During the semi-finals of the tournament, Alex described how he had a winning hold on his opponent. But just before he flipped and pinned him, a picture came into his mind of being the next State Champion. Inside, his internalized belief that *he was a loser and would never amount to anything* caused him to startle at the discordant sensation of seeing himself as a winner. He loosened his hold for a moment. In that moment, his opponent slipped out of the hold and proceeded to flip and pin Alex, winning the match.

This memory played out in his mind's eye in response to his desire and prayer to know the truth of why he behaved like a loser in his adult life. He had never made this connection and was amazed at what the Holy Spirit showed him. Alex opened his eyes and tears began to fill them. He looked at me and said, "That is the story of my life." He had been living out his life in accordance with the self-image he held in his innermost mind, even though he had been a believer in Jesus for years.

When Alex subsequently opened his soul to the Lord pouring forth profound words of affirmation, love, and worth, a wonderful shift happened. Alex let the Holy Spirit do a thorough exchange as he renounced and released the lie of being a loser, followed by an inflowing soul-realization that His real Father thought of him as a winner.

The lie of being a loser had been deeply embedded, and it took more than one session before Alex was willing to release this belief and forgive his father. But once he did, and once he allowed God to do His intended exchange, he wept tears of joy and relief as much as he had wept tears of pain and despair in our first session.

His self-image changed from a picture of himself as a *loser* to one of himself as a potential *winner*, and his God-image shifted to a personal God who loved him and had destined him to win and to be successful. Alex began to live out his life in a new way, with a new identity.

The Issue of Self-Worth

The issue of self-worth comes up frequently in both secular and Christian counseling offices. Narcissism is an excessive evaluation of self, but narcissists don't perceive that there is any distortion in their self-image; they usually don't seek help. The usual perversions of a healthy self-image are more in the downward direction of shame-based loathing of oneself. Many seek help for the pain caused by these negative evaluations.

The traditional therapeutic response to this self-hatred (which is often at the root of anxiety disorders, depression, addictions, abuse, anger, etc.) is to try to raise one's self-image by injecting massive doses of self-esteem and self-love. However, self-esteem is a satisfaction and confidence in *oneself*, and self-love often implies loving what we are, apart from a relationship with God. This is the way I viewed the problem of self-worth for years, trying to assist patients, and myself, by downloading doses of positive self-esteem—as though *esteem* was a measurable substance. Most of my "solutions" were variations of self-hypnosis . . . If you tell yourself repeatedly (using the power of positive thinking) that you are wonderful just as you are, you will gradually begin to believe it. Like so many of my self-help strategies, these efforts were futile.

At age 42, when I encountered my heavenly Father for the first time, my mind was cluttered with conflicting beliefs about myself and God. I started out in life seeing myself as privileged and superior. After I left the seminary, I had internalized a view of myself as way down on the self-worth scale. Then, as a New Ager, I narcissistically considered myself to be a "10" on the scale because of the belief of my supposed inherent divinity and goodness. It took several years for God to untangle my snarled perceptions. As I released these conflicting views and exchanged them for truths spoken directly into my heart by the living Word of God, a new awareness dawned quietly in my soul: Worth is a relational reality, not a measurable substance.

The Presence of a loving Father gradually crept into my life. As I accepted the offer of Jesus to "Abide in Me and I in you" (John 15:4), God conferred worth on me by loving me in demonstrable ways, confirming the reality that I am His child and friend. But I could only have that sense of worth by being in relationship with Him. I was the son in Jesus' Prodigal Son story (Luke 15:11-32), the son who returned to his father, received his embrace, and began to live out his days as a son in relation to his father.

I had indeed been a *wretch,* which simply means a person who is in deep distress. I had filled the God-shaped space in me with everything but God and had remained a wretch like the prodigal son in the pigsty.

It took many years but I finally discovered that God created a place for Himself in me, that it is a design-feature of my human nature and that of the patients whose journeys I witness. It's a *relational vacuum* that is filled by the dynamic of a relationship, not a *quantitative hole* that needs a substance to fill it. When I received the reality of Him loving me, as a Father loving His son, I discovered that He had grafted me back into Himself. *A sense of worth was conferred upon me in the context of relationship.*

From the relational sense of worth that I now experience in living out my days as a son of my Father who is Lord of all, I believe that a quantitative self-worth scale is a false framework. To say that I am intrinsically good and have eternal worth and value in and of myself, apart from God, is not true. It is also not true to say that I am a miserable wretch who is worthless.

I have come to believe that part of being created in God's image is an embedded relationship-design: To be complete, and therefore *whole* and of worth, is to be relationally connected to Him. As framed in Augustine's prayer, "You have made us for Yourself, and our hearts are restless until they rest in You."

Self-Worth According to Jesus

In Luke 18:9-14, Jesus tells a parable about a Pharisee and a tax collector. The Pharisee bragged that he had achieved high *worth* in himself by doing good deeds. In total contrast, the tax collector, acutely aware of his actual state of emptiness, kept his eyes downcast and simply called out to God to have mercy on him, an abject sinner. This is not another of Jesus' castigations of the Pharisees for hypocrisy. It is more a statement about the Pharisee's mistaken notion of self-worth and Jesus' revelation of the actual human condition of all mankind, personified in the parable of the tax collector.

It took years for this truth to make its way into and through the layers of deception in my soul, but by God's mercy and love the veil fell from my eyes and I realized that *I am the tax collector*. Paradoxically, the journey to the Lord conferring worth upon me began by an acknowledgment of my self-inflations of pride and arrogance, my stubborn defiance and disrespect of my Father, and by realizing the utter spiritual emptiness of my soul. The real journey to having worth began by declaring spiritual bankruptcy.

As I truthfully recognized my poverty and, as the "tax collector" that I was, called out to God, He responded to my plea and my brokenness, and grafted me into Himself. *Then* I had real value, as did the prodigal son when he returned to the embrace of his father and lived out his days in the family to which he belonged.

Both the prodigal son and I technically might have been of noble birth, but that fact alone would have been hollow had we remained in our wretchedness. It is true that "God doesn't make junk." We humans junk up His creation. I would certainly have continued doing so had I not returned to my Father, to live out my days as His son.

Chapter 10

The Heart of Transformation

In the last two chapters, I have described how interacting with God has been a key component in my transformation, and how these in-depth interactions with God have dramatically shifted my soul into a realization of my true identity as a beloved son of a gracious God. In this chapter, I will share with you my discovery of the fountainhead from which the springs of transformation flow. By doing so I intend to clarify the nature of *exchange*—the word that points to the heartbeat of transformation.

The Great Exchange

During the writing of my first book, *Healing Troubled Hearts*, it became clear that the activity of inner healing ministry could best be described as exchanges—truth for lies, peace for anxiety, freedom replacing bondage—all of which are variations of life replacing death. Isaiah 61 clearly delineates the dynamics of these exchanges. The chapter begins with "The Spirit of the Lord God is upon Me . . ." and then reveals that this Spirit swaps out beauty for ashes, joy for mourning, and honor for shame.

All of the exchanges come from this same Spirit of God as He "heals the brokenhearted, proclaims liberty to the imprisoned, and gives relief to those weighed down by heavy burdens." These exchanges by the Holy Spirit are precisely what happens in inner healing sessions with brokenhearted, depressed, and anxious persons who come for healing.

Further, these verses in Isaiah 61 are actually a *foreshadowing* of Jesus, the fulfillment and full truth of all these exchanges. For many years the verses of the Bible that have literally given me shivers are in Luke 4:16-21. Jesus had just returned from 40 days of fasting and

..1 the desert. He walked into the synagogue of Nazareth on the Sabbath day and was handed the scroll of the Book of Isaiah.

Standing up to read, He immediately went to Chapter 61 and began, "The Spirit of the Lord is upon Me . . ." and continued reading the passages about healing the brokenhearted, setting captives free, and unburdening those who are oppressed (v.18).

Then (this is the part that always gets to me) He handed the scroll back to the attendant and sat down. A pause followed—everyone was looking at Him. Jesus said to them, "Today this Scripture is fulfilled in your hearing." In other words, He was saying that the "Me" of "The Spirit of the Lord is upon Me" was Himself! Can you imagine sitting in that hushed synagogue when this event occurred and Jesus said that?!

Understanding the very mission of Jesus as a fulfillment of the Isaiah 61 passages about "healing the brokenhearted," and exchanging "beauty for ashes" and "joy for mourning" has led to an understanding of what real inner healing is all about. I now use the term, *Divine Exchange Inner Healing*, to describe this ministry.

And further, I have been led to see that the exchanges that bring healing are actually part of the whole magnificent process of reconciliation with God, as described in 2 Corinthians 5:18: "Now all things are of God, who has reconciled us to Himself through Jesus Christ, and has given us the ministry of reconciliation."

The following paragraphs comprise a brief story of how my eyes were opened to this understanding:

One day, while doing research for *Healing Troubled Hearts*, I was reading the *International Standard Bible Encyclopedia* concerning 2 Corinthians 5:18 and made an astounding discovery: the Greek word for "reconcile" is the same word used for "exchange." I wondered, how can this be?

Here is how I believe this can be: *Reconciliation* is a term of *relationship.* In Matthew 5:23-24, Jesus says that if you have a broken relationship with a brother or sister, "First be reconciled to your brother" before presenting an offering to God. The process of reconciliation involves two individuals removing obstacles in their relationship by *exchanging* thoughts, feelings, and apologies if necessary . . . with the goal of *removing all* alienation and misunderstanding, and *replacing* them with restoration of fellowship.

The significance of reconciliation between God and mankind is seen in 2 Corinthians 5:18-20, and Ephesians 2:12-16, where we find an intensive form of the word for exchange/reconciliation (*apokatallasso*). Through the death and resurrection of Jesus, there is a transformation of the relationship between mankind and God—from being broken and alienated, to restored and re-attached to Him. It is evident that Paul had the meaning "exchange" in mind in 2 Corinthians 5:21 when he wrote that God "made Him [Jesus] who knew no sin to be sin for us, that we might become the righteousness of God in Him."

While pondering this Divine Exchange, with the Bible and the *Bible Encyclopedia* open before me, a long moment of absolute awe enveloped me. I knew that I had come upon the heart of the Gospel! I was perched at the fountainhead from which Springs of Life flow out to all who would be reconciled to God. Since that time of pondering, I have continued to feel immersed in a fathoms-deep mystery of truth that reverberates through my soul like the peal of a pure silver bell.

The next morning, after my research discovery, I fixed my eyes upon a crucifix and the Lord spoke into my heart that the Exchange is simple: **He died my death (alienation from God = death) so I could have His life. He became sin (ways of death) so I could become His righteousness (life). He died so I could live.**

Facets of the Atonement Diamond

As I now view it, Redemption is God's story. It's about *His* ultimate intentions. The whole panorama is about Him, for Him, by Him, and in Him—especially *in Jesus*. There are Scriptures about Jesus being "The Lamb of God who takes away the sin of the world" (John 1:29), and "in Him [Jesus] we have redemption through His blood, the forgiveness of sins" (Ephesians 1:7). So the phrase in 2 Corinthians 5:21 that "He made Him who knew no sin to be sin for us" certainly refers to the substitutionary, atoning sacrifice for the vast number of wayward, self-serving, evil intents and actions of mankind cascading

[handwritten: LETTING GO: "TOO PAINFUL TO HOLD", "NO VALUE LEFT TO KEEP"]

down through the centuries. The sheer weight of that cumulative corruption is stupefying.

I do not comprehend the magnitude and significance of Jesus' self-sacrifice, other than knowing that it was very costly to a holy God. But because it is so clearly and repetitively mentioned in Scripture, I accept that in *God's* mind Jesus' sacrificial death is intrinsic to the pardon and forgiveness of my sins. The old hymn intones the words, "Jesus paid it all," and many believers use these words to express the essence of Jesus' redeeming sacrifice. In the first years after my conversion experience, I could not fully receive this forgiveness; but once I released the lie that I had "gone over the limit" in my sinning, God's forgiving embrace gathered me to Himself in a new and wonderful way. This *facet of forgiveness* is wondrous indeed.

[handwritten: SHAME]

However, it has taken many years for another precious facet of the Atonement Diamond to flood my soul with its radiant light: Sin is not only wrong *doing*, it is also wrong *being*. Sin is a determined and deliberate detachment from God. For years after my conversion, I thought my prideful, rebellious self could be cleaned up and corrected. I reverted to old religious instructions about *dying to self* as meaning that *I* needed to deal harshly with the arrogant, stubborn, selfish side of my nature—as though I could either discipline it into good behavior or squash it. *[handwritten: COLOSSIANS 3...]*

Finally, the Holy Spirit encouraged me to hold my gaze upon the distinctive feature of this second precious facet: that Jesus took upon Himself my *heredity of sin*, that is, the disposition of self-realization, self-indulgence, and self-independence which tries to make sure that I remain in the pilot's seat of my life. **This dominant disposition is my "God-wannabe" and it can't be cleansed, corrected or killed by me. It has already been sentenced to death and has *already died* in Jesus on His cross.** *[handwritten: "I HAVE ALREADY BEEN CRUCIFIED W/ CHRIST..."]*

Herein is revealed the facet of transformation, a facet that is at the heart of everything I have been given to say in this book. If "Jesus paid it all" captures the core kernel of the facet of forgiveness, "Jesus took it all" encapsulates the essence of this facet of transformation.

[handwritten: WHAT ABOUT THE LIE OF ESCAPISM OF OLD/NEW ATTRACTIONS — BECAUSE THERE; IS A SENSE OF PLEASURE THAT I DO NOT HAVE AT THIS MOMENT. I AM AWARE OF WHAT I LACK/DON'T HAVE RATHER THAN GRATEFUL FOR WHAT I DO HAVE?]

Jesus took upon Himself not only all the sins of the world, but also the entire counterfeit sin-nature of mankind.

The resplendent light from this second facet of the Atonement Diamond has burned into my life from these verses: "Or do you not know that as many of us as were baptized into Christ Jesus were baptized into His death? . . . knowing this, that our old man was crucified with Him, that the body of sin might be done away with, that we should no longer be slaves of sin. For he who has died has been freed from sin" (Romans 6:3-8).

For a long time I didn't want to take this death-plunge because of my life-long attachment to self. But finally I experienced the nature of the Spirit as a relentless, consuming Fire. Acknowledging the death of my old self in Jesus has opened the way to receive my new self, which is the resurrected life of Jesus in me (Ephesians 4:22-24 ESV). *[handwritten: EGO]*

Here is my sense of what constitutes the *facet of transformation:* *[handwritten: REALLY]*

Jesus came into the world, and for the first time ever a human being lived a totally righteous (rightly aligned with God) life. But as this righteous God-Man lived out His life in truth and love, He was confronted by the world, the flesh (self), and the devil—all of whom hate God and everything for which God stands. It was war: Love against hate.

The world. The Roman Empire was a graphic picture of the ways of a corrupted world—envy, power, greed, and the forces of dominance and enslavement used to maintain power. Here we find the epitome of the old self's proclivity to survive by any means, without concern for anyone else. *[handwritten: TO TAKE...]*

The flesh. Both the ways of the world and the flesh can be seen in the Jewish rulers' corruption of religion for self-gain. Jesus repeatedly challenged their deception, hypocrisy, and superficiality. At Jesus' trial, the ways of corrupt human nature were further on display through the Jewish rulers' hatred and lying, and the fear-laden mob— so easily persuaded by lies in order to gain favor with their rulers.

The devil. Behind it all was the personification of hatred of God. Here is the source of pride, lawlessness, and rebellion, intent on destroying God's creation and anyone aligned with God. Although possible only because of God's permissive will, Satan orchestrated the whole concoction of forces pitted against Jesus by using and manipulating anyone who ate and savored the same pride-permeated lies which exuded from Satan himself.

At the cross on Calvary, Jesus took upon Himself this whole mess ... not only the perverseness of what was inflicted upon Him there in Jerusalem, but also the *entirety* of mankind's perverted actions and attitudes. He took them all onto the cross and hosted them in His body, soul, and spirit. What poured onto Jesus on the cross was the totality of humanity's existence as separated from God—pride, envy, lust, self-centered anger, hypocrisy, violence, and all the corruption and evil that has wormed its way into life on this planet since the Fall.

What also poured onto Jesus was the totality of the hurtful human *wounds* inflicted upon one another from living for centuries apart from God: pain, shame, fear, abandonment, rejection, and abuse of all sorts.

Jesus suffered. Gruesome were the wounds inflicted on His body. Unspeakable were the shame and pain of being naked on the cross, and being ridiculed and rejected by those who had known Him. Horrific was the loneliness He felt when the sins and entire sin-nature of the world were heaped upon Him (Matthew 27:46).

What I see on the cross is the ugly face of a counterfeit, corrupted "human nature" (including my own), blindly heaping hatred and insult on a Person who was both a holy God and a righteous man.

In Jesus' suffering, we see the wrath of the devil and of sin. I believe that suffering and pain are expressions and built-in consequences of sin. The powers of evil inflicted the suffering on Jesus, which God allowed because of His overarching plan. The fallen human self was on graphic, brutish display. Here on the cross are the results of mankind's cumulative existence apart from an abiding relationship with God. Here is the fruit of "I did it my way"—total disrespect of God and an attempt to snuff Him out.

But this Day of Atonement was also the beginning of the Day of the Lord.[7] Sin tried to pull Jesus down and destroy Him, but God executed judgment on sin once and for all, because the righteousness of Jesus swallowed up and ended the reign of sin and death. He died, but He gave up His righteous spirit to His Father (Luke 23:46), and God raised Him up out of death. Death had no claim on this sinless, righteous man.

On the cross, Jesus gathered up into Himself the entire corrupted nature that had begun in Adam, and He plunged it to judgment and death. *Here* we see God's wrath: in His judgment and execution of sin. God's anger has always been against sin and evil, not against us. Like a loving parent who hates the cancer that has spread its vicious tentacles into His children's lives, He has taken action to exterminate the soul-eating cancerous growth of sin. And He has given us the healing, cleansing balm of Jesus' Risen Life to replace the death-dealing cancerous "nature" of sin.

Sin didn't take Jesus to death as a final state of being, though it tried. Jesus took our sin-nature to death. Once again, the penetrating light of Romans 6:6: ". . . knowing this, that our old man was crucified with Him, that the body of sin might be done away with, that we should no longer be slaves of sin."

It was a cosmic war between good and evil. On the cross, in Jesus, sacrificial and holy Love triumphed over hatred and evil.

What Jesus did on the day we call Good Friday brings to my imagination an old story, which I am adapting here for purposes of illustration: I see a powerful creature inhabiting a lagoon that was once a beautiful lake but is now called "the black lagoon," because this evil creature has poisoned the waters of the lagoon with his malice and hatred. All who drink of the water become painfully poisoned and are dying. A *Superhero* arrives on the scene, plunges

---

[7] See **Day of the Lord** entry in Bromiley, G.W. (ed.), *The International Standard Bible Encyclopedia*, Vol. 1, p. 879: "The entire conception of that day [The Day of the Lord] centers therefore in Christ and points to the everlasting establishment of the kingdom of heaven, from which sin will be forever eliminated."

into the lagoon to confront the evil creature, who jumps on Him and tries to claw, bite, and drown Him to death.

The Superhero sustains many wounds as they thrash about in the water. There is an eerie, silent moment in which the battle is over, and it appears that the Superhero has succumbed to death, that He is finished. But He rises victoriously and it is clear that the Superhero has overcome the evil creature, completely defeating him. The Superhero cleanses the lagoon of the poisonous hatred, and the waters are restored to their original pristine beauty.

An additional vitality infuses the entire situation because the Superhero remains living in the lagoon. He stays so that all who come to Him can be healed and cleansed of the toxins they had ingested. The lagoon is more beautiful and life-giving than ever before.

We usually think of Jesus on earth having "superhero" status because He was God. But in His *humanity,* as well as by His Divinity, the destructive powers of evil (including the corrupted human nature) were vanquished by the God of all power and might.

Good Friday was the turning point of time. The Incarnation began in a stable, found visible expression in the Crucifixion and Resurrection, and now extends into human hearts whenever a person opens up to receive God's gift of His Life in the Divine Exchange He offers.

This Exchange has been happening within me since that Sunday in Brightmoor Tabernacle in 1984. At the time, I was disconnected from God and swimming in the poisoned waters of the black lagoon. I was lost, enslaved, lonely, just reacting to and coping with the circumstances of my life, like a hardened survivalist. Now, after more than 30 years of living within the dynamics of the Divine Exchange, my life is radically different. I am being healed and restored by drinking the Water of Life . . . and His Life-giving Springs flow through me to others.

Chapter 11

Exchanges for a Lifetime

Earlier in my life, whenever I heard the words of Jesus, "I am the Vine, you are the branches . . . Abide in Me" (John 15:4-5), I pictured Jesus saying these words at the Last Supper. However, I have discovered that Jesus' invitation to "Abide in Me" is an invitation to engage with Him at Calvary by agreeing to let die in me what died in Him through His crucifixion and death. Yes, He died *for* me, and effected reconciliation to God and forgiveness of my sins. He also died *for* me in the sense that He overcame and brought to judgment my pseudo-human nature because I was utterly incapable of overcoming it myself. *→ EGO ?*

It was my *old self* that was judged and put to death on Jesus' cross. I have accepted Jesus' invitation to join Him there and be crucified with Him in this sense. And this acceptance of death has also been the way to receive His Life: "If we have been united with Him like this in His death, we will certainly also be united with Him in His resurrection" (Romans 6:5). *THIS LIFE I LIVE IN THE FLESH I LIVE BY FAITH...*

"*United* with Him like this in His death" has an etymological sense of *grafting* within it. In the grafting process, such as a branch grafted into the main stem of a grapevine, the host stem and the branch to be grafted are cut in such a way that they fit exactly into each other. When graft and host are fit together, they are bound with a cloth so that they can grow and fuse together. The sap of the vine then flows into the grafted branch and enlivens it.

When I accepted Jesus' invitation to abide in Him, at first it was based on a realization of my deep need for forgiveness. But as I immersed myself into the reality of who He is and why He came to Earth, the ravages of my sin and soul-wounds began to call out painfully. I needed rescue and deliverance from entrenched self-centeredness and its consequences; and I needed healing from traumas inflicted upon me by myself, by others, and by life-circumstances.

Many times now I have brought to Him the shame and pain of soul-afflictions, releasing them onto Him . . . knowing that there is a unique place in Him cut exactly in the shape of any affliction I might have. I let my afflictions and sorrows fit into Him, this "Man of sorrows" (Isaiah 53:3), *releasing* them to Him, and then I *receive* His resurrected Life (Sap) from Him, the Vine.

In this place of meeting, of abiding, I have also brought to Him the burden of my sins, confessing them and then receiving the truth that He has already taken these sins upon Himself on the Cross and disposed of them.

For me, the cross of Jesus is now a *living* reality, not a *lifeless* symbol. I encourage recipients and patients to abide in Jesus there, when the Holy Spirit opens the way to receive healing in this manner. I have also found that an exchange can sometimes take place rather quickly in unstructured inner healing moments in daily life.

For instance, a judgmental attitude towards a person may jump into my mind in certain situations. I have felt the reality of "I have been crucified with Christ" (Galatians 2:20) in such a situation, and have said either to myself or aloud, "be crucified" to the attitude, and I release it. Sometimes in such a moment, an image of the cross comes to mind and, like an iron filing pulled to a magnet, the released judgmental attitude flies to the cross, where it truly belongs. Then the Holy Spirit brings an attitude of compassion from the very character of the risen Jesus to replace the old-self attitude, as Sap from the Vine flows into the vacated soul-space.

When I interact with the Lord during dedicated prayer times, the purpose of quieting my mind is to receive an awareness of His Presence. As I feel led, I open to a passage in the *written Word* and begin asking the Lord to connect me with Himself, the *living Word*. My desire is for Him to show me whatever He wishes me to focus on, and then to show me whatever He wants me to know about that focus. I seek communion with Him first, spirit to Spirit, giving permission for Him to release His Truth, His Love, and His life into my soul.

Healing moments often occur during these prayer times as the Holy Spirit reveals some part of my old, dark self that has been hanging on, not yet fully accepting that it belongs on the cross. The release/receive dynamic takes place in these moments as I allow the Lord to make His exchange in my soul. And the same exchange takes place in moments during the day, as described above, when an ugly or afflicted part of my soul shows its face. I don't always take the time for an exchange, but when I do, relief and peace follow.

However slowly, the relationship with my Lord grows, as does His Life within me . . . decision by decision, exchange by exchange. I am being reconciled, restored, redeemed. One day it will be fully so, including my body, ". . . the Lord Jesus Christ, who will transform our lowly body that it may be conformed to His glorious body" (Philippians 3:21).

These releasing and receiving exchanges are also the place of healing for Divine Exchange Inner Healing Ministry. Based on 2 Corinthians 5:21, "For He made Him who knew no sin to be sin for us, that we might become the righteousness of God in Him," I encourage patients to meet Jesus in this place of abiding. In any given Divine Exchange session, the Holy Spirit clarifies the transaction that is ready and ripe. *Ripe* = the Lord's will and a recipient's willingness for exchange.[8]

The following is a visual representation of the Divine Exchange process:

---

[8] See Chapters 15 and 16 of *Healing Troubled Hearts* for guidelines and steps of Divine Exchange Inner Healing Ministry.

DIVINE EXCHANGES
Our Father Reconciling us to Himself

For He made Him who knew no sin to be sin for us, that we might become the righteousness of God in Him.

2 Cor. 5:21

RELEASE	RECEIVE
guilt, condemnation	forgiveness, full pardon
separation from God	regeneration, reconciliation
captivity, addiction	freedom, new attachment to God
fear	trusting in God, peace
lies	truth that sets free
sorrow	joy
pain	comfort, healing
shame	cleansing, sense of belonging
curses	blessings
old thoughts, emotions, desires	mind, emotions, will of Jesus
troubled, anxious, agitated	calmed by His love...true peace
weighed down, burdened	Jesus carrying our burdens
self-reliance	God-dependency
self-protection	the Lord my shield
bitterness, resentment, hate	the forgiving heart of Jesus
critical disposition	His heart of compassion
self-ownership	grafted in as sons and daughters
defeated, despairing	overcoming in Christ Jesus...hope
self-will, stubbornness	humility, alignment with God's will
lust, jealousy	content with God's provision
greed	satisfied by fullness of life in Him
impatience, desire to control	willingly yielded to God
doubt	the faith of the Son of God
oppressed by Satan	deliverance, standing in Christ Jesus

Handwritten annotations:

SOMETIMES I NEED SORROW

NOT SOMETIMES ALL TIMES DO I NEED JOY?

BOTH GOOD / IMPORTANT TO HAVE

GIVES OUR LIMBIE SYSTEM DEGREES OF

ALL IN REASON

WORK OUT YOUR SALVATION WITH FEAR & TREMBLING

GRATE FUL

- In the diagram, the Heart is the love of the Father, the Source of God's intent of reconciling us to Himself. Within this Heart is the mission of Jesus to carry out the Reconciliation, via the cross and then the infusion of Jesus' risen Life into human hearts by the Holy Spirit. The terms of the Divine Exchange are delivered in the words of 2 Corinthians 5:21. *[handwritten: VERY GOOD WAS/G GOD now Corruption]*

- In the words under RELEASE, I have listed some of the many manifestations of the old self, the *old man* that Jesus pulled down into death. The cross is a living symbol, representing Jesus Christ Himself as the Crucified One. The cross in the diagram signifies Jesus drawing all wounds, curses, and sins unto Himself as they are released and confessed to Him for healing and cleansing. *[handwritten: THE NEW MAN USES EMOTIONS APPROPRIATELY]*

- The words under RECEIVE are the aspects of Jesus' Life that a person receives as the Holy Spirit (the Dove) orchestrates an inflow of Truth, Love, Goodness—Jesus' nature—to replace what has been released. It is a *Divine* Exchange because the Holy Spirit does it, and because Jesus' Life is imparted.

- The horizontal infinity sign in the diagram depicts the exchange process. This sign represents the dramatic shift that takes place within a person's heart. Within these transformative exchanges, the Finished Work of Jesus (so clearly recorded in 2 Corinthians 5:21) is realized and actualized in the ongoing sanctification of individual lives.

- A final observation about the diagram is that **as the Divine penetrates and interweaves with the human through the dynamic of releasing and receiving, both healing and transformation take place . . . They go hand in hand**. This will become clearer in Part III, coming up.

While looking over this diagram, a memory surfaced of an inner healing session I facilitated years ago. I will briefly describe it as a way of demonstrating the diagram.

The patient was a young woman who had to live overseas for an extended period of time because her parents were missionaries. She left behind her best friend, and the aching pain of this separation increased rather than abated as the months passed. She began manifesting symptoms of depression from the sorrow in her heart, and had lost interest in daily activities.

As we approached the place in the healing session in which the recipient is encouraged to listen for how the Lord wants to minister, the image of Jesus on the cross came into her mind. It became clear that the Lord was inviting the young woman to release her sorrow to Him because He had already taken it upon Himself so many years ago.

Previously in her life, she had developed a trusting relationship with the Lord and responded now to His invitation by being willing to release her sorrow to Him. After she did so, she began to receive a flood of love and comfort flowing into her heart, mind, and body. Some moments passed and she began to feel the companionship of the Lord Jesus right there with her, a closeness that was new and palpable. The image of Vine and branch grew vivid for her, and she spent a few minutes soaking in the experience of abiding in Him, being grafted into Him, receiving Life from Him. The aching pain gradually ebbed and was replaced with a comforting peace.

Months later I found out from her parents that her depression had lifted and she had resumed daily activities with her usual zest for life. It is likely that, in a new way, she was also experiencing Jesus as her steady companion and ever-abiding friend, maybe even her best friend.

A note on radical change. Before ending Part II, there is a matter to clarify that is both theological and practical. On numerous occasions I have heard and read an interpretation of 2 Corinthians 5:21 as indicating that we receive Jesus' righteousness (right standing with God) and that we have no righteousness of our own. I fully agree. However, the usual analysis then proceeds with the assumption that this is a *static, unchanging situation*—as though Jesus covers us with His righteousness like putting a silk garment on a pig. But we humans are created in God's image and likeness, and however corrupted and fallen human nature has become, we are not pigs.

As will become clearer in PART III, I firmly believe that God's will for us involves healing and transformation; *He just doesn't want us trying to transform ourselves by our puny, futile self-efforts.* Jesus' righteousness covers us <u>while we cooperate with God in absorbing</u> <u>and assimilating the nature of Jesus</u>, as we intertwine with Him in the releasing/receiving relationship described in Part II.

[handwritten margin notes: IN DAILY WALK; US TO EXPERIENCE NOW; CAUSE; IT HAS ALREADY BEEN DONE]

What Jesus did *for* us on the cross, He wants to do *in* us now. Yes, God loves us as we are, but He loves us way too much to let us corrode away in our old-self juices. He fully intends to change us, as we are willing, into the image and likeness of Himself that He created us to be.

Those who receive by faith the Person of Jesus are "partakers of the divine nature" *now* (2 Peter 1:4). PART III is a focus on how I believe "partakers" are actually being changed into Jesus' human nature, and how this change is also a journey of becoming one's true self.

[handwritten: HOW ABOUT AS OLD CELLS DIE?]

Returning to the image of vine and branches, observe that as the grafted branch grows into the host vine, all old cells of the branch die; they are replaced by new cells as the life-giving sap continuously flows into the branch. The branch slowly but surely becomes part of (one with) the vine, and is literally a new creation.

[handwritten note: ARE THEY REPLACED WITH THE EPI GENETIC DNA OF A NEW LIFE FORCE CREATED BY THE TRANSFORMING OF THOUGHT FROM THE MIND OF CHRIST?]

PART III

The Intention of Transformation

Chapter 12

A Treasure Uncovered, A Treasure Unclaimed

In Chapter 10, I mentioned a marvelous facet of the Atonement Diamond that is most often held up as the distinguishing feature of Christianity: God's forgiveness of our sins. As the sacrificial Lamb of God, Jesus removed the guilt associated with all human wrongdoing and replaced it with God's full forgiveness. In the first two chapters of PART III, I will bring more fully into the light what I spoke of as another facet of the Atonement Diamond, the *facet of transformation*.

Forgiveness is a gateway to freedom, the start of an adventure of living in a new realm—the Kingdom of God. However, transformation is God's solution for the evil that has infested His creation. As Scripturally depicted in Chapter 10, the *facet of transformation* has within itself God's way of dealing with the pervasive depravity of our deeply flawed human nature.

There is a static complacency suggested in the supposedly Christian bumper-sticker: I'M NOT PERFECT, JUST FORGIVEN. Yet, Jesus says, "Therefore, you will be perfect, as your heavenly Father is perfect" (Matthew 5:48). In this chapter and in Chapter 13, I hope to clarify what Jesus meant by this statement and, at the same time, let shine more brightly the powerful, personal, transforming dynamic I call *the forgotten facet of the Atonement*.

The Forgotten Facet: A Treasure Uncovered

The American evangelist D.L. Moody was once walking along the banks of the muddy Chicago River, contemplating how salvation and sanctification work together. In the distance, ahead of him, he saw a small group gathered in a circle, looking down at the ground. As he approached, he saw a man lying on his stomach in the middle of the group. Someone was kneeling in front of him, pressing on the man's upper body, trying to resuscitate him. D.L. Moody looked at this man who had just been pulled from the river and saw dirty water running out of his nose, mouth, and ears.

Instantly it became a picture of the issue he had been contemplating. In *salvation* a person is pulled from the river of death and his/her spirit-life is enlivened. The "muddy water" that entered a person while in the river has to be pressed out—representing the life-long restoration process of *sanctification*. This "dirty water" is expelled from the soul and life-giving "oxygen" streams in to replace it—the Holy Spirit filling in the vacated places in the soul.

Analogously, I understand my experiences as follows: (1) At Brightmoor Tabernacle, I had received and responded to the invitation to "be reconciled to God" by a profession of faith in Jesus. The Holy Spirit came to dwell in the innermost sanctuary of my being. I was quickened and enlivened—a new creation. I had been pulled from the river of death. I was alive. I was saved. (2) However, the ways of death ran deep within my body and soul. In a sense, God didn't have all of me yet; I was just beginning to let His ways replace my ways. The first two chapters of this book give graphic details of *muddy water* that needed to be pressed out of my soul.

In this dirty water were layers of lies, lusts, false interpretations of life-experiences, hidden resentments, and doubts about God's goodness. In addition, I had provided safe harbor for patterns of living by my own wits, self-devised strategies for surviving, self-protective defense mechanisms, victim attitudes of blaming others, and ingrained modes of rationalizing, deflecting, and outright denial.

My soul and body had existed for many years apart from a living connection with God. They were stuffed with self-centered ways—my soul alienated from God by defiant pride, and my body bound to the earth through unrestrained sensual appetites. All of these ways of the self were not immediately changed out in my soul when I was pulled out of the river of death and enlivened by the Holy Spirit. However, the Lord was now within me to accomplish the changing out, insofar as I was willing to let Him do so.

In the previous chapter, I presented the Scriptural fact of the Divine Exchange: Jesus taking on all our sins and our sin nature, and giving us His nature in exchange (2 Corinthians 5:21). Now, fusing that fact with the imagery of the river of death and its muddy water, I see the dirty water as not just a minor nuisance to deal with, but as a highly toxic substance that must be removed in order for full health to be restored.

For the first years after I had been pulled from the river of death in 1984, I oscillated between feeling a complacent satisfaction of being saved and anxiously trying to figure out how to get the muddy water out of me. I was walking around hacking and coughing on the gunk, as I began to vomit up all the self-serving ways that had constituted my lifestyle up to 1984. My first knee-jerk reaction was to energetically strive to get healed and holy (reading books, applying strategies . . . trying trying trying). Finally, I began to rest in the Potter's hands and let Him change me His way.

I now recognize that there is an ancient aspect within me (my corrupted self) that cannot be reformed or transformed. It always wants its own way and it always will. **I choose either to let that aspect assert itself or I choose to stay in agreement with God's perspective that in Jesus this self has been crucified.**

The Forgotten Facet: A Treasure Unclaimed

I am a minister and psychotherapist, believing fully that the pain, sorrow, and shame lodged in my soul and in the souls of my patients comprise much of the "muddy water." However, the reality of our own sin is also part of the muddy water. Wounds and sin are often intertwined.

A case comes to mind in which a woman patient had been verbally and emotionally abused by her mother during childhood. The trauma left a murky quagmire of shame, fear, anger, and resentment in her soul. During inner healing sessions, she released the pain and fear (wounds) to the Lord, receiving comfort and peace in exchange. Then she released the anger and resentment (sins) she had harbored for years through a spontaneous, heartfelt confession to God. As soon as she released the resentment, compassion for her mother filled her soul.

My patient had been a Christian for years and had tried many ways to deal with her pain and resentment. She had developed what I call a *survivor-self,* a mindset and stance in life's circumstances that are structured and formed by the belief: *I have to take care of myself because no one else is there to help.* The abuse from such a primary caretaker as her mother had broken her capacity to trust anyone, including God. So as a Christian, she was unwilling to give up her own survival solutions, until she became desperate for a solution that would work.

When she came to the end of herself (her own solutions), she finally was willing to move through her fear and to trust what God had in mind for her. What she discovered by coming out of agreement with the lie that *she had to take care of herself* was that God had a new life in store for her, a life of knowing freedom and joy. She began to let go of her old survivor-self and to trust God, believing 1 Peter 5:7 AMP for the first time: ". . . casting all your cares and anxieties upon Him, for He watchfully cares for you." She wrote me a letter two years after her inner healing sessions:

Starting the process of inner healing was a bit daunting for me. I guess when things got overly dark in my life I was willing to step out in courage. Jesus says, "Come to me . . . I am gentle and humble in heart, and you will find rest for your souls" (Matthew 11:28-29). That is the Jesus I found as I entered the inner healing experience. As I was prayerfully drawn back to painful childhood experiences, it was a great relief to regain those moments while releasing the associated hurt and bitter feelings. As I experienced the presence of Jesus with me in the pain, knowing He removes the shame and doesn't add to it, I was able to start a new journey in my life toward facing truth and not living with suppressed pain. The most dramatic change has been in my relationship with my mom. Everything about her used to anger me, but now I can love her and enjoy her as she is. It is amazing how forgiveness changes everything!

After completing *Healing Troubled Hearts*, in which I recounted such stories of healing in myself and in the lives of patients, it began to dawn on me that **Divine Exchanges, which were the centerpiece of the book, were not only descriptive of a significant ministry through which the Lord heals human minds and hearts, but these same exchanges were also descriptive of the whole process of transformation.** The muddy water was not just wounds to be healed, or sins to be forgiven; our whole wayward nature constituted much of the murkiness in the water. *WHAT is THAT WAYWARD NATURE BUT*

Something broadened in my thinking as I prayed into the matter. I received a sense that the Lord was stretching me to consider that what He intended for human lives had a deeply transformative thrust. He gently led me to observe the changes He had set in motion in my own life, and it became clear to me that the words of 2 Corinthians 5:17 are not dramatic hyperbole: "Therefore, if anyone is in Christ, he is a new creation." Those words speak a vivid sense of truth and life.

I observed the foundational identity changes within my personality. For several years, my identity as a son of a loving Father had been growing through the inner healing exchanges I had received. But now, in 2014, shortly after the publication of my book on the ministry of inner healing, the words of Galatians 2:20 began to radiate a more expansive understanding of Paul's Holy Spirit-inspired statement: "It is no longer I who lives but Christ lives in me."

This "new creation in Christ" named Bill Day is a hybrid of Jesus and me (I will develop this thought in a coming chapter). I began to know in my heart that God's plans for me went beyond healing. A more expansive understanding of His plan broadened into seeing the interconnection of healing, wholeness, and holiness. I saw that His plan encompasses me as a *person* who is to be radically and totally changed by abiding in the *Person* of Jesus. In this dawning awareness, the seed was planted that has grown into this second book.

In Chapter 8, I told the story of the limiting mindset in the game of basketball that considered the rim as an impassable ceiling, likening it to the limiting mindset I had in my relationship with God. I now live and move freely in an interactive relationship with the Lord; but within this interaction I have discovered another glass ceiling, this one

A REFRAMING OF HOW WE ARE DESIGNED TO PROTECT OUR SELVES...

serving as a barrier to entering fully into the dimension of transformation. Two aspects comprise this invisible barrier: *fear of losing my old self* and *the persistent power of my old self*. I will describe how these forces have tried to discourage me from plunging into the dynamics of radical change.

Chapter 13

Barriers to Transformation

First Barrier: fear of losing myself. Towards the end of the previous chapter, I spoke of "a more expansive understanding" of Galatians 2:20. This understanding was invigorating, but it was laced with fear. All of my individualistic, self-contained senses of myself felt challenged to the max. The narrow sense of self that was so well established in my thoughts, beliefs, feelings, and actions (deeply grooved patterns developed during several decades of life) resisted the radical transformation which the Lord opened before me in this new vision.

I was afraid to let go of my old sense of self and let the Holy Spirit *totally* have His way. The words of Jesus in Matthew 16:25 spoke out in a challenging way: ". . . and whoever loses his life for My sake will find it."

I know of a man who had a dream about Jesus. In the dream, the Savior's bleeding body was upon the cross, but there was another form alongside Jesus' body—an ugly, loathsome thing, the features of which the man could not make out clearly. Later, after waking from the dream, while listening to a sermon about becoming one with Jesus, the Holy Spirit revealed to the man that the ugly thing on the cross was himself, i.e., his old self. In that moment the man realized that Jesus came to terminate the corrupted creation in him, not patch it up.

Part of the fear of letting go is a fear of dying, of losing my life as I know it. It's not easy to step through this fear and face the inescapable reality of the Gospel: that the place I meet Jesus and am united with Him is on His cross. It's a place of death. In Chapter 11, I quoted Romans 6:5, "If we have been united with Him like this in His death, we will certainly also be united with Him in His resurrection." Life follows death in God's Kingdom, in Jesus and in me. Abiding in

Jesus as a branch in a vine is an agreement to let die in me the false human nature He hosted unto death while on the cross.

For many years I minimized this full understanding of the cross, out of a fear of letting my old self be acknowledged as dead . . . tolerating instead the insistence of this self that it be allowed to continue living, even to dominate. During those years, I looked at His cross and only saw Jesus as the Lamb slain to pay the penalty for my sins, but I didn't see there the ugly, malformed perversity of my corrupted human nature.

In the D.L. Moody story, the striking image is of a man saved from death *so he can live*. Having the toxic, death-water pressed out of him and replaced with life-giving oxygen is part of the saving process. Holding onto a truncated understanding of forgiveness is like pulling a drowning man out of a river but letting him lie on the ground without resuscitating him. Both pulling the man out *and* resuscitating him are part of the *saving*.

Yet, isn't this lack of real resuscitation what we do in so many of our churches? I believe that we have settled for so much less than God has offered and intends . . . by playing church, engaging in religious activities, and using our own strength to try to be "Christian."

Or, on the other end of the spectrum, participating in churches that foster thrill-seeking experiences of "Holy Ghost power." The focus there is often on tapping into the Holy Spirit to bring about God's "promises" for comfort and earthly prosperity. Through this latter lens, God becomes a celestial errand boy, a power-source to do *our* bidding.

At either end of the spectrum, the reality of death and new life is overlooked, as is the primary purpose of the Holy Spirit: *to bring to full expression the reality of Jesus Christ in human lives (John 16:13; 14:6)*.

It becomes clearer to me each day, that God is calling us to a "total home makeover" that includes replacing corroded pipes, rotten timbers, and mildew-engulfed drywall. It also includes a painful tearing apart of the entire living area of the house, enlarging it beyond its narrowly confining walls. I believe He calls us to invite Him into our hearts so He can actualize His victory over the evil *in us.* The good news? It's the work of the Holy Spirit, not our self-effort, that accomplishes this "makeover." He who calls Himself Lovingkindness wants us to trust Him.

Perhaps this image of a total makeover carries within it a clue as to why it is so difficult to step into a relationship with God in which radical change takes place. Can you feel the fear in the image of your own house being torn apart? I have encountered this fear-steeped shiver: that the radical change of dying to my old self entails a tearing apart of my very being and I will never be the same again. It is a fear of self-annihilation, that who I am will disintegrate. A scary feeling swirls around that thought of disintegration.

I have concluded that the "new creation" *is* a *new* creation, and that it's true, I won't ever be the same again. But I have discovered that the life the Holy Spirit gives to replace my old self is far better, and more *me* than my old self (What I mean by this last statement will be clarified in the remaining chapters.).

It has felt like the exercise of letting go and falling into the waiting arms of a person standing immediately behind me. There is a fear of falling, but the many-layered healings I have received in the past 30 years have built a substantial trust in God's goodness, enabling me to let go. As I write these words today, I can tell you that I have chosen to let the Lord have His way with me in the transformation He has in mind for me. I am all in.

The difficult part has been choosing to trust while experiencing the teeth of fear. Nevertheless, in any given moment, whenever I choose to trust God and actually fall more fully into His transforming arms, courage and peace flow in like a gentle tide, dissolving the fear and gently washing me forward toward the next steps He has in mind.

Second Barrier: the persistent power of my old self. In most of the patients I have seen over the years, and certainly in myself, there has been an observable aspect of the soul that develops from emotional trauma and injury. This aspect takes on a protective role as part of a reactionary belief, often formed after soul trauma: *I cannot trust anyone else, I have to take care of myself.* This protection-belief held a dominant position in my life and I was wary of trusting anyone, including God.

Through my interactions with God and the healing exchanges of inner healing ministry, this protective aspect released its power, along with the belief that it was in charge of taking care of me. I received in its place the true belief that *God is my shield and He will be present in every situation to take care of me.* A protective aspect remains in my soul but no longer has dominant or controlling power. It is now a servant, not a dictator; it recognizes the true King, the true Protector.

However, there is a disposition in me that wants to act independently of God or anyone else. It wants to control and to dominate by having its own way in all circumstances. Scripture calls it the "old man," the "old self," or the "carnal mind." It will never yield nor give up what it thinks are *its rights.* I have discussed it in Chapter 10 as a *false* human nature; it was put to death on the cross because it is not of God and never will be. Romans 8:6-7 states the matter succinctly: "For to be carnally minded is death, but to be spiritually minded [of the Holy Spirit] is life and peace. Because the carnal mind is enmity against God; for it is not subject to the law of God, nor indeed can be."

This *God-wannabe* in me has had lifelong repetitions of acting independently of God as I learned to survive on my own, coming up with my own solutions and strategies to make my way through life's struggles. My old self has held so much power that it still seems amazing how well God works out complex situations in my life without my control and manipulation!

So, commingled with the aforementioned fear of letting go is the persuasive and persistent power of my old self, which strives to stay alive. Together, these barriers have been formidable forces that have constructed a "glass ceiling." This false ceiling holds many believers back from entering the dynamic dimension of transformation, an immersion wherein lies real freedom, real life, and true Christianity.

Many folks sit passively and complacently in church pews, Sunday after Sunday. Many live in the information trap I spoke of in Chapter 7—the deception that information equals transformation. Many believers engage in religious activities that consist mostly of intellectually absorbing spiritual information and advice about how to live better lives—maybe even acting on some of this information. *But they never enter the actual transformation process that takes place in a relationship with Christ Jesus.*

I have been such a soul-dabbler. But now, whenever I am willing to go through the fear and let go of some ugly thought, or when I resist and release the Siren-call of my old self wanting its own way, a remarkable discovery occurs. The righteous life of Jesus Christ flows into the vacated places in my soul and I receive features of His nature. I can feel the change happening on the inside, moving outwardly into how I live my life.

As I said in the **Introduction**, "A wondrous treasure lies buried in the depths of the Gospel. Many know of this treasure but do not realize that it is an *interactive* treasure, to be personally engaged with and related to, not a gem to be stored away in a vault." I firmly believe that God's invitation is for us to plunge into the reality of the facet of transformation within the Atonement Diamond, a true treasure given to us from a generous God.

God's Intention: The Treasure is Meant for Us

Sorting through the Scriptures and my own experiences, I believe that the corruption within me is a *mal-formation* that has resulted from a chronic *mal-orientation*—focusing on self instead of on God and on fellow humans. My many behavioral malfunctions (sins) have stemmed from this malformation. I see in Jesus a perfect formation of spirit, soul, and body that has resulted from an *orientation* that is totally directed to God instead of to self. Being centered in His Father in every moment, Jesus received into His human nature the full download that God intended in His original creation of all mankind. God's design for human beings was and is perfectly realized in Jesus. Jesus' *right*eousness is His *right* alignment, His *right* orientation, to God and to people.

Our transformation, then, is to be a re-orientation, a re-formation, a re-creation—a new creation in Jesus. The right human orientation and formation exists only in Jesus. When we allow the

Holy Spirit to draw us into the forge of transformation that is the Lord Jesus, we are plunged into a Person who lives to realign and set free everyone who comes to Him. *Free* means *to be what we were intended to be.*

I believe that God's *ultimate* intention is the realization and restoration of His *original* intention when He made us in His image and likeness (Genesis 1:27). This restoration has taken place in Christ Jesus and takes place in those who are in Him. The first barrier I mentioned above, that is, fear of letting go and fear of trusting God's exchanges for me, is a barrier to becoming all that I am meant to be. And the second barrier, a resistant inclination to stick with my ways and my self-containment, is actually a force that holds back a shift into my true self, which is a self that resides in Jesus' righteous life.

I have concluded that this metamorphosis in Jesus is the very stuff of life, the adventure that my heart has always longed for. The treasure that has been uncovered has emerged from a hidden realm and now glows vibrantly and invitingly. It's as though I had been asleep in a spell and had forgotten the promise of God to take away my stony heart and give me a new heart in exchange (Ezekiel 36:26). Now I am awake and I see that God has been faithfully fulfilling His promise. The new heart He has promised is the heart of Jesus in me.

In the Introduction of this book, I said that I would be exploring the question of whether or not a person can really undergo a transformative process in which he or she actually *becomes* the likeness of Jesus. By Scripture and by my experience, I can unequivocally answer "yes." But it still seems amazing. Jesus' heart is not just a treasure, His heart is the crown jewel.

THE fleshly HEART IS A HEART of stone
A SPIRITUAL HEART IS A HEART OF FLESH
A HEART OF flesh was an
ORIGINAL DESIGN

A LIMB of Jesus...

Chapter 14

Grafted into the Vine

During the past 30 years, as I have interacted with God and taken the plunge into His transformative process, the truth stated in 1 John 4:19 has deepened within me: "We love Him because He first loved us." Listening to His love-invitation to live in Him and with Him, I am overwhelmed by the degree of personal intimacy offered in this invitation.

Fear and Awe

As I let the fullness of God's invitation reverberate through my soul, I encounter another seeming barrier of fear, but this fear *draws* rather than repels:

"Let all the earth fear the Lord; let all the inhabitants of the world stand in awe of Him. For He spoke, and it was done; He commanded, and it stood fast" (Psalm 33:8-9).

God spoke Himself into human flesh (John 1:1-14). **He came to live in humans in a new way so that we can live in Him in a new way.** But the invitation to "become partakers of Christ" (Hebrews 3:14) is so in-your-face personal and intimate that it's scary.

Did you feel any fear-laced awe when I described the grafting process of Vine and branches in Chapter 11? Jesus' "Abide in Me" is the awesome invitation of a holy, mighty God intimately and personally drawing us into Himself. *Fear-laced* because such an invitation to abide in the Lord God seems too good to be true. Who am I to participate in such an awesome relationship as the invitation suggests?

As I let the details of that Vine/branches image (John 15:4-5) make their way into my soul, I am gripped by the reality emanating

WORK OUT YOUR SALVATION W/ FEAR & TREMBLING

YES, THERE IS A BENEFIT / OF THE BRANK OF NEW GROWTH! CHARACTERISTIC OF THE UNIQUENESS TO THE

from the image. As the grafted branch stays bound to the Vine, old cells are continually dying off and are being replaced by new cells. The old sap (an old-tree residue crusted into the interior of the branch) gradually dries up and flakes away, and Sap from the new Vine flows in, giving Life to every cell in the grafted branch.

The branch literally becomes one with the Vine. More and more the branch resembles the Vine because it is actually being made into the same substance as the Vine to which it is attached. No longer is the branch an *outsider* but now an *insider*, a real member of the Vine. The embracing, intimate love of such a transformation is scary awesome when I let it fully soak into my soul.

Or how about the invitation of Jesus in John 6:53-56?

Most assuredly, I say to you, unless you eat the flesh of the Son of Man and drink His blood, you have no life in you. Whoever eats My flesh and drinks My blood has eternal life, and I will raise him up at the last day. For My flesh is food indeed, and My blood is drink indeed. He who eats My flesh and drinks My blood abides in Me, and I in him.

Here is another up-close-and-personal invitation of deep intimacy. On the natural plane, when we partake of food and drink, they are absorbed, assimilated, and gradually transformed to become life in every cell in our bodies. Jesus uses this image to make it clear that He offers to be in us in a real and substantial way.

The image conveys the spiritual reality of Him in personal union with us. Note that the image of eating His flesh and drinking His blood is not a metaphor to express anything fanciful, or a hyperbolic embellishment to highlight an idea. Jesus said, "the words that I speak to you are spirit, and they are life" (v.63).

Physically, flesh and blood comprise the whole body. Blood especially is seen as the carrier of life. *Spiritually*, flesh and blood mean Jesus' Life. It is an astonishing image of personal intimacy and union, and it is to be taken literally ("spirit and life" literal): "He who eats My flesh and drinks My blood abides in Me, and I in him" (v. 56).

THY WORDS WERE FOUND & I DID EAT THEM & THEY BECAME A JOY & THE DELIGHT OF MY LIFE.

What does it mean to eat Jesus' flesh and drink His blood spiritually? It suggests a process that is personal, whole-hearted, and full of life-altering transformation. Hearers and readers can reject the image (as many of His disciples did) as a strange, cannibalistic-sounding metaphor. Or, it is possible to codify it into a lifeless concept "intended" by Jesus simply to take relationship with Him seriously. Or, we can allow the image to speak *spirit and life*, as Jesus said, receiving its fullness into the inner recesses of our souls.

In doing the latter, I have concluded that true belief in Jesus is much more than mental assent to the existence and truth of Jesus Christ. True belief is all-in immersion, as attested to by Paul in Galatians 2:20: "It is no longer I who live, but Christ lives in me." **Eating and drinking Jesus means taking Him into our very being so fully and willingly that we let the Holy Spirit transform us into the Christ-like men and women God intended us to be.**

In these images of Vine and branches, and eating and drinking, Jesus unambiguously declares that life-altering transformation will be the result of *believing* in Him by *abiding* in Him.

Searching for True Spiritual (Trans)Formation

Back in the 1970s, I tried to *abide in God* by sinking into the aching emptiness of my soul through meditation, believing I would eventually reach the deep spiritual springs that supposedly exist in every human soul. I found instead a self-absorbing introspection that was devoid of any "Enlightenment."

In churches across our land, the reality of the need for Jesus as Savior is fading away, finding a place only in the scenes depicted in their stained glass windows. In several modes of *spiritual formation* that have crept into churches, contemplation supposedly produces transformation. The process is one of sinking into yourself until you realize the "truth" of your oneness with God. This oneness is supposedly transformative. It is as though transformation happens by a mystical process of spiritual osmosis.

In this understanding, there is no need for a radical change that affects one's very identity. Meditation supposedly reveals an already-existing union with God within human nature. There is no perceived need for being saved or delivered by an external power (like a Savior). Mankind can supposedly break through the chaotic dysfunctions of life by sinking inwardly beneath the fray in meditation, or plow through life's challenges by God-designed human potential that lies within our grasp.

For me, this is a New Age vision and it is a mirage, a delusion, a nostalgic dream of returning to what could have been. Paradise was lost and we cannot go back by going within ourselves to find it. I also believe that retaining any semblance of connection to this nostalgic, backward-looking vision blinds us from soberly seeing and grasping the total makeover that is warranted for human beings to be what God intends us to be.

However, there is a way to restore God's intentions for Paradise. There is a way that we can commune deeply with God. There is a way to partake of divinity and become our true selves. There is a Way.

The Way of Jesus

Meditation is Scriptural, no doubt about it. The Psalms have many references to meditating on God and on His Word. Prayer and fasting are mentioned throughout the Bible and are validated by Jesus, who Himself sought solitude and silence. But the clear context for all of these spiritual practices is *relationship*—between God as a Person and humans as individual persons. And always, God is God and we are not God. Yet He wants to share His nature with us and has made provision to do so.

The following paragraphs of this section express the understanding I have arrived at about the provision God has made for us to participate in Him:

~

God created a space and a place for Himself within us as a design-feature of our human nature. We are made in His image and likeness so that we can attach to Him and engage with Him in ways that are compatible and companionable with His nature. God breathed His life into all of us when He created us. He continues to breathe His love into us in every moment, if we will receive it. I say "receive it" because love is a relationship, not a *force* or a *substance* in some subterranean reservoir in human souls. **Humans are not inherently God or in possession of divinity. We are inherently designed to be in relationship with God and to have His image and likeness come alive within that personal relationship.**

We can see evidence of God having breathed His life into us. Calamities such as earthquakes and hurricanes elicit this breathing as we witness sacrificial and voluntary acts of service. Various circumstances can call forth bursts of heroism, compassion, and goodness, drawing out what God has planted within us as likenesses of Himself.

Even in our normal daily lives we see evidence of persons seeking and acting on something within—an inner urging that looks to the needs of others, not only oneself. That is the urging of love and it's at the very core of being created in God's likeness. The Bible tells us that God is Love. He is also Justice, Forgiveness, Mercy, Wisdom, Goodness, and Truth. We see evidences of all these attributes in the daily course of living as well, but I think of them as so many candles in an enveloping darkness.

Like deep-sea divers cut adrift from our air hoses, we have cascaded down through the centuries, generation after generation, passing on the toxins of self-absorption, self-gratification, and inclinations to iniquity that have resulted from being cut off from the life-giving *oxygen* of fellowship with God.

Is there a more empirically verifiable reality on this planet than the pervasiveness of human depravity? We experience it every day, within us and around us. For 40 years, in my counseling practice, I have witnessed the inner turmoil of normal, everyday folks who have been made crooked and dysfunctional by the abuse or control of others who were intent on having their own way—no matter the cost to others.

Then the hurt persons act out their own afflictions upon others, often passing them on in the same manner. I have yet to meet a person who doesn't have a sack of rocks, each sack loaded with guilt, shame, anxiety, anger, sadness, and weariness from carrying the load. Some adapt and learn to handle the load, but many stay buried under the weight and become depressed, or afflicted with other maladies of soul and body.

Yet there is something within us that balks at accepting our human afflictions as deep or substantial. The *denial* of radical corruption blares out from a self-protective place in our souls where we try to salvage a semblance of self-worth. I lived in such denial for decades and have seen this phenomenon in many patients.

Bookstores have shelves devoted to self-worth and self-esteem— how to build self-confidence and develop the power to create your own successful destiny in life. They claim to teach how to overcome all obstacles and become a winner by your own power. "It's within you, just tap into it and pull it out," say the many authors, as if in unison.

My experience has been that, far from finding God buried deep within me, I finally was willing to acknowledge my own "sack of rocks" buried deep within me. After almost 20 years of immersion in Humanism and New Age, I was soberly awakened to my own brokenness—not awakened to Enlightenment.

I experienced unfathomable poverty of spirit. And in that place of dire need, God showed up to tell me who He is, and to invite me to partake of Him, to come into relationship with the Person who is the Way, the Truth, and the Life. I never discovered a dozing divinity in my New Age days, but from 1984 forward, I discovered that I had been *dozing in denial* of how wretched my life really was and how badly I needed to be rescued.

Abiding in Him as a branch in the Vine is first of all an acknowledgment of a deep need for forgiveness and reconciliation with God, and a recognition that my entire "old man" must die and be replaced with Jesus. Picture a gardener cutting off a branch that had been growing on one tree, and grafting the branch into the trunk of another tree. By being grafted into a new tree, the branch undergoes death to its old life and experiences regeneration from the life of its new tree. In a way, you could say that a newly grafted branch is *born again* and is a *new creation* (John 3:7; 2 Corinthians 5:17).

Such an understanding of "Abide in Me" is far removed from the understanding that has been brought into Christ's church by New Age influences. **We participate in God by accepting Jesus' invitation to come into His Kingdom through the portal of His death and resurrection. Once in the Kingdom, the continuous exchanges that take place there are the continuous acts of dying to old life and receiving new life.** Each day it seems that the Lord shows me more clearly that to abide in Him is to participate in the continuous cycles of releasing death and accepting life, until He comes.

Imitation or impartation?

Looking at the Beatitudes in Matthew 5, there seem to be some very high standards that Jesus sets: "Blessed are the meek . . . . Blessed are the merciful . . . . Blessed are the pure in heart" (v. 5-8). Couple these with Jesus' directive to "love your enemies . . ." (v.44) and "be perfect, just as your Father in heaven is perfect" (v.48). Or consider Mark 12:29-30, when Jesus sums up God's laws as loving God with your whole heart, soul, mind, strength, and your neighbor as yourself. For good measure, add in Peter's injunction ". . . but as He who called you is holy, you also be holy in all your conduct" (1 Peter 1:15).

If I have to meet these standards in my *self*, by my striving, I may as well cry out like Isaiah, "Woe is me, for I am undone" (Isaiah 6:5). None of these directives and standards can I meet in my natural man, in my old human nature.

I have concluded that all of these directives are spoken to the life of Jesus in me. He is the only human capable of meeting these standards, and only He-in-me can realize these requirements.

Much of contemporary understanding of what it means to be a Christian is to follow Jesus, to imitate Him (What would Jesus do?), and to be a student of His teachings. I believe Christians are to be *apprentices*, in the classic sense of this word, not students. A student learns concepts and skills from a teacher, then adapts and applies them to his own life. An apprentice *becomes* what his master is. He enters the master's world and emerges like the master himself.

The substance of the master (his wisdom, his secrets, the essence of his craft) is internalized by his apprentice, such that there is a kind of replication of the master in the apprentice who surrenders to him. An apprentice doesn't just *imitate* his master; in a real sense the master *transmits, imparts* himself into his apprentice.

In an even more real sense than a natural master and apprentice, by abiding in Jesus in the ways I have described throughout this book, I believe that we are *apprentices* who are actually becoming expressions of our Master. This is a significant way in which spreading the Kingdom of God on earth takes place. Jesus *is* the Kingdom, and as I internalize more of who He is, He and His Kingdom become more incarnated in the world. I am to be a city on a hill, and a lamp stand, from which His Light in me shines out to everyone I meet (Matthew 5:14-16).

This is not a "let go, let God" passivity but a process of God's transformative actions working together with my choices to participate. Let's say I have critical thoughts towards an acquaintance, George. I confess and release these judgments (and receive the Lord's forgiveness), and then I ask the Holy Spirit to show me how Jesus sees George. I meditate on the Person of Jesus, not on an emptiness within my soul.

By the power of the Holy Spirit, I see, sense, or hear that Jesus loves George and is wooing him to Himself. I choose to release my old-life attitude and let the Lord exchange it with His loving attitude towards George, thereby allowing the mind of Christ within me (1 Corinthians 2:16) to manifest outwardly. As I treat George with love instead of judgment, Jesus is a bit more present on the Earth, now through me, a member of His body (1 Corinthians 12:12). However small a step, the Kingdom of God advances in that moment.

Cocoon or Chrysalis?

In the 1970s and 1980s, there was a New Age worldview that employed the image, "cocoons of Light." The image conveyed the thought that if enough people came together and meditated deeply, a kind of critical mass could be achieved and we would burst our cocoons and soar into a planetary, evolutionary leap in global consciousness.

In this New Age "cocoons of Light" image, the life within the cocoon was considered to be the inherent Divine Energy that is within us by our very nature, the so-called "God within." Bursting forth from the outer casing of the "cocoon" would supposedly be humans who have evolved to a more advanced state, leaping ahead to the next level of "conscious evolution."

I think this image represents the *God-wannabe* in our fallen human nature, still succumbing to the temptation to become God-like by its own devices.

On the other hand, a butterfly chrysalis is a place of transformation. I believe that by being in Christ Jesus we are in God's chosen *chrysalis* for us; and the transformation therein is as radical as the caterpillar-to-butterfly metamorphosis that happens within a chrysalis. This in-Christ chrysalis is not a cocoon of human spinning but is a dynamic site of God's choosing, in which real transformation occurs. It is His redemptive, restorative plan to return humanity to the journey-course He intended for us in the wisdom of His original design.

The key difference here is that the Christ-chrysalis is God's plan for advancing *His* Kingdom and realizing *His* intentions, rather than the consciousness-cocoon of humans advancing *their* kingdom, creating *their* own reality. Bottom line: Transformation is God's idea and power, not ours.

This metamorphosis takes place in humans as they are "conformed to the image of His Son" (Romans 8:29) and "transformed" (2 Corinthians 3:18) into Jesus' image. Transforming happens by *conforming* and *forming*, "until Christ is formed in you" (Galatians 4:19).

Succinctly, **Christian spiritual formation is the formation of Jesus in us.**

C.S. Lewis had a poignant perspective on the matter, which points to the radical nature of our metamorphosis in Christ Jesus:

It is something like that with Christ and us. The more we get what we now call 'ourselves' out of the way and let Him take us over, the more truly ourselves we become. There is so much of Him that millions and millions of 'little Christs,' all different, will still be too few to express Him fully . . . . In that sense our real selves are all waiting for us in Him. It is no good trying to 'be myself' without Him . . . . Until you have given up your self to Him you will not have a real self.[9]

The story now shifts into an exploration of what it means to be conformed to and formed into the likeness of Jesus Christ. Up to this point, I have described original creation as having been marred beyond repair. What does it mean to be *re-created* in the image of God by becoming the likeness of Jesus, who is the perfect and "express image" of God (Hebrews 1:3)? As "little Christs," we are to be as He is. Who is He in His human character and personality?

The exploration of this last question will be a way of viewing the blueprint of the persons we are designed to become. Jesus is the master paradigm of what it means to be a *real* man or woman, that is, persons who actualize God's original design.

---

[9] C.S. Lewis, *Mere Christianity* (New York: McMillan Publishing, 1952), pp. 189-190.

Chapter 15

Original Design

As I absorb God's Word and continue to interact with Him, something like a Copernican shift is taking place in my soul. In this analogy, similar to a realization that the sun and not the earth is the center of our solar system, a realization deepens in me that the Bible unveils a plan in which God is the center, not humans.

We know that God's thoughts are not our thoughts (Isaiah 55:8), and that God has had a blueprint in His creative heart of love "before the foundation of the world" (Ephesians 1:4); but we tend to see history only back to Creation and the Fall. And we only see history as far forward as the apocalyptic visions of the apostle John.

But God's intentions were in His mind before the Fall and beyond end-time visions, into the endless ages that are to come. I believe that one day the warp of self-preoccupation will be fully exchanged for a capability to have a God-centered view of reality; but for now I pray for the Holy Spirit to open my eyes *to see,* as I abide in His Light more and more.

There is much written on the subject of the *imago Dei,* the image of God, and the presentations are many-sided. I have come to some conclusions, but I acknowledge these conclusions as exploratory and incomplete, afloat as they are in the vast sea of sacred mystery, God's heart.

In possibly the greatest of all mysteries—that God could and would become human flesh (John 1:14)—we have a way to see what God intended when He created humans in His image and likeness. In the Epistle to the Hebrews 1:3 ESV, we are told that Jesus is "the express image of His [God's] person . . . ." So when we fix our eyes on Jesus, what we see and hear in Christ Jesus is what God intended for mankind. By looking at the attitudes, character, and actions of Jesus in His humanity, we can see human life from God's perspective, not from our human-centered view.

In these last five chapters of the book, my hope is that something of God's ultimate intentions will emanate through the words and yield an overarching, God-centered viewpoint.

Created in God's Image and Likeness

"So God created man in His own image; in the image of God He created him; male and female He created them" (Genesis 1:27). "And the Lord God formed man of the dust of the ground, and breathed into his nostrils the breath of life, and man became a living being" (Genesis 2:7).

The Genesis 2:7 passage paints an intimate picture of a Face-to-face imparting of life. In the Genesis 1:27 depiction, we have an expression of gender equality from the outset, yet an indication that the different characteristics inherent in masculine and feminine are all God-endowed. It is not difficult to sense that something special and unique has taken place in this creative event.

One further passage rounds out the picture: "Then God said, 'Let Us make man in Our image, according to Our likeness; let them have dominion over the fish of the sea, over the birds of the air, and over the cattle, over all the earth and over every creeping thing that creeps on the earth'" (Genesis 1:26).

Three items to note in this passage:

- "Let Us make man . . ." strongly indicates that God does not exist as a solitary being. God is relational in His very essence. What is hinted at here is developed in the New Testament when Jesus speaks of His relationships with the Father and the Holy Spirit.

- There is no significant difference between *image* and *likeness.* Throughout Genesis, sometimes one or the other word is used rather than both together, such that they seem to be almost interchangeable. They are perhaps combined sometimes to add intensity to the thought that man is a being who is like God in certain respects.

- In having dominion (stewardship, authority) over the animals and over all the earth, we can possibly infer that this is an aspect of the image of God, Who has supreme and ultimate dominion over the earth. Certainly having "dominion over" has a sense of rulership, but as God's representatives, humans are also to be caretakers of the earth and all that is in it.

Digging deeper into *image and likeness* yields graphic meanings such as the stamp on a coin or the mark made by a seal—like the image of the seal that is pressed out onto clay or wax. The image carries the form and features of the original stamp or seal.

The root idea of the Hebrew word translated *image* is that of a *shadow*. *Image* also can mean *reflection*, such as a mirror capturing the reflective image of a person. *Likeness* connotes similarity, resemblance, having almost or exactly the same qualities and characteristics. "He is just like his father." "She has a remarkable likeness to her mother."

The text of Genesis 1 makes it clear that mankind alone was created in the image of God. Unlike the other creatures, only men and women bear a special resemblance to God. What are the characteristics peculiar to humans that liken them to God? What is it that distinguishes mankind from the rest of creation? Some clues may be found in what God has revealed about Himself; and some clues may be found in capabilities that differentiate mankind from the rest of creation. Let's look at some of these clues.

1. Thinking, Feeling, Willing. Although God is spirit (John 4:24), He is described throughout Scripture as thinking (e.g., Psalm 139), feeling (many references to God feeling anger, grief, joy, and other emotions), and willing (creating, intending good, choosing to forgive). We cannot say we have exactly the same capabilities as God, but we have them in a *uniquely different* way than animals and the rest of lower creation.

Although animals have a measure of understanding and can be trained to respond, they are not capable of conceptual thought and high-order abstraction. Animals can think but not the way humans do.

The same is true of emotions. Animals can feel, but the range of emotions that can be evoked in humans is qualitatively different. Compassion, joy, and the various emotions that arise in response to art or beauty or tragedy are not found in animals. And the difference between instincts (animals) and willful choice (humans) is not even on the same continuum. The human capacity to choose has destiny-shaping power, a power certainly closer to a divine than an animal attribute.

2. Relationship Capacity. Returning to Genesis 1:26, the relational aspect of God as three Persons in one Godhead is a significant aspect of being made in God's image. God is not a solitary Being, nor are humans. I believe that when Jesus identified loving God and loving neighbor as conditions for inheriting eternal life (Luke 10:25-28), He was describing essential ways we have been hardwired to be like God.

Many qualities come into play here when speaking of relational capacity: a sophisticated level of communication involving the complex use of language, emotional expression, reasoning, speaking, and willful choices.

Also coming into play is the reality of *person.* Clearly, God is presented throughout the Bible as having personality. Whether Father, Son, or Holy Spirit, God reveals Himself as having specific attributes and characteristics. So too with humankind, we are persons with distinct personalities.

The significance of *person* is its qualifying concept that each "I" be distinct and unique. The nature of relationship requires that there be separate persons who can exchange their own unique thoughts, emotions, and desires in the back and forth of dialogue, and in the reciprocal giving and receiving involved in relationships.

At the outset, mankind was equipped to enter into trusting relationships with God and with one another—Person to person with God, and person to person with one another.

3. Moral Capacity. Of all creatures upon the earth, only mankind has the ability to choose between right and wrong. The sense of moral responsibility, called *conscience,* is clearly patterned after God who is just and righteous (Psalm 89:14), good (Mark 10:18), and holy (Isaiah 6:3). God's perfectly holy nature is the basis upon which right and wrong, and good and evil are determined. As God succinctly stated the issue in Leviticus 11:44, ". . . and you shall be holy; for I am holy." Perhaps an amplifying paraphrase could be: "You were made in My image and I am holy, so you too shall be holy."

4. Spirit Imprint. Men and women have God-given spirits that return to Him when they die (Ecclesiastes 12:7). As stated in Acts 17:28, "For in Him we live and move and have our being." The immortal spirit given us by God certainly makes us image-bearers of Him who is called "the Father of spirits" (Hebrews 12:9).

An aspect of God's spirit imprint within each person is the desire to reach toward and relate to God. Anthropologists and sociologists alike have found that man alone possesses an inherent religious inclination. The evidence points to something planted in human hearts, a sense of incompleteness and a desire, a hunger. Ecclesiastes 3:11 says that God "has put eternity" in our hearts.

Perhaps theologian Augustine of Hippo captured this trait of human nature best when he said, "You, O God, have made us for Yourself, and our hearts are restless until they find rest in You." I have always felt the ring of truth in this oft-repeated statement of Augustine. A corollary of this assertion is that the human desire for God mirrors God's love for us, because the reality of love has reciprocity within its nature.

What if one of the elements God breathed into the human organism was an ever-present messaging unit in the human genome that finds fulfillment only in human hearts beating as one with the heart of God?

More characteristics of being made in God's image could no doubt be added to this list, but just naming these four aspects provides insight into what seems to be part of God's plan: to fit and equip us for fellowship with Him and with one another.

The Image of God: Destroyed or Dimmed?

I begin this section with a clarification. Bear with me here. Although closely related and intertwined, I detect differences between *human nature* and the *image of God* imprint. Simply, human nature means that we are beings composed of spirit, soul, and body. Being divine image-bearers means that we have unique and highly advanced capacities to think, to feel, to will, to enter into intimate relationships, to discern right from wrong, and to desire God. *Nature* refers more to our composition, *image-bearer* refers to the intrinsic structural capacities and imprints that permeate this nature.

Re human nature: Entrenched orientation to self has led to disfiguring character *malformations*, resulting in *malfunctioning* in every area of human endeavor. The world now is dimmed, dulled, and deadened. I believe that Scripture bears out God's verdict on the human nature inherited from our fore-parents: It is corrupted beyond repair and has been judged, one day to be totally eradicated. God decided that our maimed natures could no longer support and carry to completion what He intended for us.

Re image of God imprint: After perusing various resources, including Scripture, I have concluded that the image of God in mankind has not been annihilated but rather perverted by mankind's fall away from God into the self-idolatry called sin.

Many achievements—smart phones, space travel, modern medicine—show that God has endowed His image and likeness beings with stunning capabilities of creative thought and action. However, the self-slant of corrupted human nature shows up unmistakably in human beings in the massive waste, exploitative use, and disgraceful pollution of our precious natural resources. We have devolved into careless caretakers and selfish stewards of the earth.

In the realm of relationships, there is certainly evidence of large-scale dysfunction, perversion, and abuse. Deterioration is obvious in the moral morass resulting from the wide-scale decimation of objective standards of morality, but we still have the imprint of relationship capacity.

A BOLD STATEMENT IN BOLD PRINT

Perhaps the deepest disfigurement of God's imprint on us can be seen in the rampant spread of secularism (a denial of God's spiritual imprint), but time after oppressing time the cry of the spirit-dimension within us rises to the surface to be heard and satisfied.

However diminished and perverted God's imprint in human nature has become, God's Word does not portray the image of God as completely destroyed. For example, in Genesis 9:6, God tells Noah that murder is wrong: "For in the image of God He made man." Also, in the New Testament, long after the Fall, James speaks of mankind, "who have been made in the likeness of God" (James 3:9). These verses indicate that the image of God has not been destroyed.

I believe that God breathed a long, deep breath into us (Genesis 1:26), and **His likeness within us is more pervasively a part of us than our corrupted nature.** But centuries of entrenched malformation have so dimmed and thinned God's Love-filled, Light-filled, Life-filled breath in us that a rescue operation was inevitable. Like an artist whose *opus magnum* has been horribly defaced, God could not and would not tolerate such an affront to His creative genius.

Jesus was the Lamb of God and the Light of the world from before the foundation of the world (Revelation 13:8; John 1:1-9). He came into a very darkened world, but He came as God's Light, Love, and Life, to *re-breathe* God's image and likeness back into God's masterpiece work of art: human beings. The restored masterpiece is the "new creation" (2 Corinthians 5:17).

Jesus came fully into the deepest places of our human nature (Hebrews 2:17) that He might dispose of human malformation (old nature). Then, *in exchange*, He gives us a regenerated human nature (His own), and restores in us a perfect image (His own) of God.

In Jesus, God's masterpiece is restored.

As we are about to explore in the next chapter, when looking at Jesus we are feasting our eyes on God's original intention and design when He created us in His image. Over 130 times in the New Testament, the words "in Christ" or "in Christ Jesus" are repeated. Here, in Jesus, God the Master Craftsman restores the work of art He created so long ago.

Chapter 16

A Masterpiece Restored

While I was preparing to write this chapter, a vision unfolded within my mind. The vision seems to be a bridge between the previous chapter and this one, so I share it.

I saw a large tree in a garden. A prominent branch had broken off and was lying on the ground. The branch's leaves had wilted, and parasitical weeds had sprung up, wrapping themselves tightly around all of the offshoots growing out from the branch. Life was slowly being drained out of the branch by these weeds. The branch had been on the ground for a long time and rot had eaten holes through the bark, penetrating well into the interior. Various insects and other creatures feasted on the rotting parts. The weakened branch tried valiantly to survive but, however gradual, death was inevitable.

Then the large tree from which the branch had broken off began bending its entire formidable crown and trunk down towards the detached branch in a gesture of embrace. It is difficult to describe what happened next. Without detaching from the tree, a significant segment of the bending tree (branch-like but also trunk-like) reached down and enfolded the branch on the ground, gently and tenderly lifting it up and taking it to its breast. This branch-trunk partially morphed into a figure that I knew was Jesus. As the Jesus/branch folded the detached branch into Himself, He completely absorbed all the rottenness, bugs, and weeds, replacing them with His loving Life.

In the final scene of the vision, the detached branch was grafted into the tree by Jesus' embrace, and became one with the Tree-Branch (God-Man). The branch was becoming enlivened and restored, and was showing signs of resembling again its former state of being as an organic part of the tree. There was also a glimmer of understanding that, in its new state of being, the branch would grow into something better than it had ever been—better even than its original state, before it had detached.

As I ponder this vision, it seems significant to point out that there was an absorption of the corruption that had happened to the detached branch and an immediate, regenerative restoration upon being lovingly re-attached to the Tree. Life-giving Sap could flow into the branch and its offshoots. However, it was clear that gradual yet steady exchanges of new cells replacing old cells would accomplish a complete transformation in the branch—from deadened and weakened to enlivened and strong—until the branch would truly be one with the Tree.

As I experienced the conclusion of this vision, I had a sense of completion and wholeness, accompanied by feelings of peace and joy.

Fixing Our Eyes on Jesus

- "He is the image of the invisible God, the firstborn over all creation" (Colossians 1:15).
- ". . . Christ, who is the image of God" (2 Corinthians 4:4).
- ". . . His Son . . . who being . . . the express image of His [God's] person" (Hebrews 1:2-3).

From Scripture it is clear that Jesus is the perfect and sinless image of God, the pattern in whom we can see the blueprint of what God intended for mankind when He created us in His image (Genesis 1:26). The passage from Hebrews above brings into focus the graphic meaning of "image." The phrase, "the express image of His person" is more literally rendered: "the impress of His substance." Here we see the rich meaning of *that which is engraved*—such as a stamp on a coin or the image pressed out in clay or wax from the original mold of a seal. Jesus is a perfect impression/expression of God.

For those who are in Christ Jesus, it is instructive to look closely at the character, conversation, and conduct of Jesus because we ". . . are being transformed into the same image from glory to glory, just as by the Spirit of the Lord" (2 Corinthians 3:18). And Romans 8:29 speaks of us being "conformed to the image of His Son."

As we fix our eyes upon Jesus, we are at the same time identifying the design features God had in mind for us. There is no better way of seeing the image of God than to look upon Jesus. What we see and hear in Christ Jesus is exactly what God intended, and intends, for humankind; who Jesus is we are to become. As we allow Him to lift us up from our detached state to His breast, there to abide in Him, we are re-attached to the Tree from whence we came, so long ago.

So, who is Jesus? What are we to take note of in determining what and who we are to become?

1. Relationship Capacity Restored: It Starts at the Top. In Chapter 14, I named relationship capacity as an aspect of being made in God's image. Jesus demonstrates the depth of what this means. In Hebrews 12:2, a curious term is used for Jesus: "Looking unto Jesus, the Author and Finisher of our faith. . . ." The Greek word used for "Author" here doesn't mean so much one who "causes" as one who "takes the lead." In this twelfth chapter of Hebrews, Jesus is presented as the Leader of a long procession of those who had lived by faith. He is the Pattern of how to really live by faith.

Often I have had to remind myself that the *man* Jesus was like us humans in every way except sin. A life of faith wasn't automatic or easy for Him just because He was also the Son of God. He had to cultivate and develop His faith moment by moment as He walked the earth for 33 years. How did He do this? What is a life of faith?

First and foremost, it is a life lived in complete reliance upon God. Never did anyone live out so completely Proverbs 3:5: "Trust in the Lord with all your heart, and lean not on your own understanding." Over and over in the Gospels we read of Him getting up early in the morning to seek a quiet place to commune with His Father. We hear His words that He does only what He sees His Father do (John 5:19). Many times Jesus reaches up to the Father in supplication, in gratitude, and in acknowledgment of their intimate oneness (John 17).

By faith He looked away from discouragements, difficulties, and opposition arrayed against Him. By faith He resisted all temptation—whether it came from Satan, or false expectations coming from the people and even from His disciples. Out of the fullness of His own faith He told His followers to "Have faith in God" (Mark 11:22).

Jesus the man lived in <u>constant communion with God</u>. He lived out the realization that "He that sent Me is with Me" (John 8:29). From Bethlehem to Calvary He enjoyed an unclouded relationship with the Father. And after three hours of darkness on the cross, laden and saturated as He was with our separated-from-God sin, He cried out "Father, into Your hands I commit My spirit" (Luke 23:46), thereby re-establishing fellowship with His Father.

Another aspect of Jesus' everyday life of faith was His <u>obedience to God</u>. Never has anyone been so yielded to God's will: "I live by the Father" (John 6:57); "I do always those things which please Him" (John 8:29); "I have kept My Father's commandments, and abide in His love" (John 15:10).

From His dependence, His communing, and His obedience, a fourth aspect of Jesus living by faith naturally flowed: <u>an assured confidence in the unseen future</u>. "Faith is the substance of things hoped for, the evidence of things not seen" (Hebrews 11:1). Jesus was able to live *now* in the trusting realization of *what is to come*. Before Calvary, He said "I have overcome the world" (John 16:33).

What made Jesus' life of faith possible was the *trust* that existed between Him and His Father. Jesus' choice to co-mingle His will with His Father's will no doubt was based on a <u>complete trust</u> in His Father. In this reality of Jesus' complete trust, I believe we are given a way to see what God intended from the beginning when He created us in His likeness.

The Fracture of the Fall. As the story of Adam and Eve unfolds in Genesis 2, many have thought of God's command not to eat of the tree of the knowledge of good and evil as a probationary test. But the command could also have been a warning: that when His human creatures ate of that tree, a kind of poisoning would occur, and they would die. God did not say, "If you eat from that tree I will punish you by killing you."

In His love, God could have been warning them that they were free to eat of any tree, but eating from the tree of the knowledge of good and evil would produce very harmful effects. First, He knew what would happen to their relationship with Him if they *broke trust* by doubting and disobeying Him. Second, He knew what would happen if they tried independently, in their creaturely minds, to discern moral truth without first seeking the wisdom that comes from communing with Him.

Might this communion and fellowship with God be symbolized by the tree of life, standing quietly there in the middle of the garden? What is life but God Himself? And what happens if any organism is cut off from its life-source? Death.

This may be wild speculation on my part, but I have audaciously created a rendition of what might have been in God's heart, spoken not only to Adam and Eve but also to all mankind:

> I created you to have an intimate relationship with Me. I have specifically told you of another tree, the tree of life, in the middle of the garden. I have given you free will, to choose to eat of its fruit. If you focus on Me first, and commune with Me, then My Life will enter your spirits, permeate your souls, and flow into your bodies. You will receive all the wisdom and knowledge you need to live on the earth and carry out My plans for you. This is how I have arranged things. Believe Me. Trust Me.

As much as they were acts of disobedience and defiance, I believe the decisions of Adam and Eve were *breaches of trust*. We know from painful experiences that when trust is broken in any relationship, severe consequences follow. In the vision-vignette at the beginning of this chapter, the disconnected branch (lying in a separated and weakened state on the ground) is a picture of the human condition after the Fall.

Throughout the ensuing centuries, we can trace a gradual slippage of humans from relational beings to the solitary individualists so prevalent in the world today. Self-reliance has been touted as a virtue of manhood and a hallmark of independent womanhood. In truth, self-reliance is our greatest weakness. Inside this encased way of living is the pain of aloneness and deep insecurity that results from a lack of relational connection, especially the connection with God.[10]

The worst consequence of this false independence has come from the fracturing of our capacity to relate and communicate with God. We are riddled with doubts about God's goodness; seized by an urgent sense of staying in control; and plagued with myriad self-solutions to medicate the separation-anxiety rippling out from our state of detachment from God. Further, beneath this painful mess we often harbor anger at God, believing that He is not in control and that He is not adequately taking care of us.

Restoration in Jesus. Only Jesus has the relational capacity to live in trust with our Father and to maintain a life-giving connection with Him. Interestingly, in the *Original Aramaic New Testament* translation, the concluding phrase of Galatians 2:20 is rendered, ". . . I live by the faith **of** the Son of God," rather than the traditional translation, "I live by faith **in** the Son of God." I am in accord with this rendering from the Aramaic. It clearly indicates that our faith-capacity has been severely damaged, and this too must be swapped out, exchanged.

Jesus, our first-born Brother (Romans 8:29), is the blueprint of the relationship God intended for us. He is the relationship-image restored, and as we bring Him our doubts and our false senses of independence and control, He will absorb and replace them with *His* relationship capacities.

This is a capacity to commune with God daily, to depend on Him wholly, to trust Him implicitly, and to obey Him unswervingly. The capacity-exchange is ongoing in me as I write this sentence, because my capability to trust has been so badly broken. I need the Lord every day to keep identifying what is ripe to be released to Him so that I can continue growing into a man who walks with God in unswerving faith and trust.

[handwritten margin, left side, vertical: A FAITH NOT OF OURSELVES → EPH 2:]

[handwritten margin, right: ??]

[handwritten note at bottom: → HOW ABOUT OUR DESIGN NEEDS TO BE RE CALIBRATED.]

---

[10] I treat the subject of self-reliance more extensively, especially its detrimental influence on men, in *Healing Troubled Hearts*, p. 191 ff.

2. Moral Capacity Restored: A Way to Be Good. A revealing glimpse of Jesus' character is given in Hebrews 1:9, that He "loved righteousness and hated wickedness." Jesus did not just act righteously, He *loved* righteousness. He loved fairness, justice, equality. At the same time He *hated* wickedness; and we are to hate evil as well (Proverbs 8:13). We are to be conformed to Christ's character in this regard. Let's see how Jesus' moral capacity found expression.

Throughout His 33 years on earth, Jesus demonstrated what it means to be a moral human being. Time after time in the Gospels we see Him confront evil with truth, and we see Him act with love and mercy as well.

He broke religious taboos by fellowshipping with tax collectors, prostitutes, and other sinners. He ignored religious traditions in order to lovingly heal and feed people on the Sabbath. He boldly crossed prejudicial ethnic boundaries, fellowshipping with and speaking well of Samaritans and Gentiles. He socialized and touched the untouchable lepers. In the midst of an extremely patriarchal culture, Jesus treated women with remarkable dignity and respect. With boldness and love He exposed legalism, prejudice, and sexism.

However, by walking in love and truth, Jesus provoked the wrath of self-focused mankind around Him—people almost totally invested in keeping their power and having their own way. Jesus' continual confrontation of corrupt self-orientation (sin) ultimately led to His crucifixion. But even before the cross at Calvary, Jesus received death-threats, curses, ridicule, and attempts to trick and trap Him as He spoke to the crowds. *Already He was laying down His life,* unafraid to confront evil with goodness and truth.

Jesus' whole life, up to and including Calvary, was the presence of the Kingdom of God over and against the oppressive kingdom of Satan. Such is the power of moral sensitivity, actualized and made real within the perfect moral capacity of the Son of Man.

In my childhood, my mother often said, "Be a good boy, Billy" as I walked out the front door of our house. Decades of my life were spent in frustration and guilt as I tried with my self-striving to be good. I pursued this quest in many ways, and then went through seasons of abandoning the pursuit of being good, thinking it futile. **But in the last 30 years, since abiding in Jesus, a desire to be good has awakened in me in a new way. I believe this desire is part of God's image in me, awakened and enlivened by immersing my life into Christ Jesus.**

God intends His goodness, truth, and moral sensitivity to be infused into my character. *In Jesus I have discovered a way to be good*—to have moral sensitivity, to seek truth, and to be able to stand boldly in the light of truth even while surrounded by darkness and evil.

The Holy Spirit is making me good and is increasing an unflinching moral sensitivity within me by replacing the dregs of my depravity with Jesus' moral capability. Still a long way to go, but I am a work in progress, confident of the promise in Philippians 1:6, ". . . that He who has begun a good work in you will complete it until the day of Jesus Christ."

3. The Deepest Imprint of All. The picture of God breathing His Spirit-life into us when He made us, inspiriting our bodies and souls with reflections and likenesses of Himself, is a picture of multi-layered magnificence and wonder. At this moment in my story of becoming the likeness of Jesus, it feels as though we are arriving at the quintessential core of what it means to be created in God's image. From the Scriptural evidence and my own experience, this core is the most essential reality of God and of human beings: LOVE.

In the simplest of terms, the Hebrew word for love is *give*, and the word that best typifies the core characteristic of corrupted human nature is *grab*.

"God is love" (1 John 4:16), but our souls have been darkened by grabbing and snatching for ourselves. So God has poured out His Love into our hearts by the Holy Spirit, through Christ Jesus (Romans 5:5-6). In this way, through Jesus, the original intention of God that we be *givers*, like Him, is restored . . . because Jesus is the supreme human giver of all time, and we are to be conformed to Him (Romans 8:29). In Him we see true love and true humility: putting others first.

We sing about it, we write poetry about it, we know in our hearts that love is what "makes the world go 'round." In Jesus we can see the nature of love and receive His capacity of *self-giving* to replace embedded, habituated *self-grasping*. For me it has felt like an ongoing blood transfusion in which, however gradual, giving becomes more dominant and natural than grabbing. And the "joy of giving" becomes not so much a reward as a satisfying realization that **I am more myself (the God-design) when I am a giver than in any other disposition or action in my daily life.**

Looking closely at Jesus, we see Him setting a standard for love: "Greater love has no one than this, than to lay down one's life for his friends" (John 15:13). As described in the previous section on morality, Jesus laid down His life in self-giving throughout His 33 years on earth. In confronting evil with truth, Jesus manifested love for His fellow men and women. Love motivated Him to speak out against prejudice, legalism, and sexism. Then, on the cross, He literally laid down His life—the perfect convergence of humility and love.

Going back to the first section of this chapter, we see Jesus building an intimate relationship of reliance and trust with His Father, abiding in Him in such a way as to know with certainty that He was indeed loved dearly by His Father. I believe He learned this experience of *being loved* by His communion with Father God. This immersion-experience then became a reservoir of love out of which flowed a pouring out of Himself in complete self-giving.

In John 7:37-38, Jesus says, "If anyone thirsts, let him come to Me and drink. He who believes in Me, as the Scripture has said, out of his heart will flow rivers of living water." He encourages everyone to do the same thing He did, that is, He felt the deep thirst for God implanted in His human spirit, and He drank deeply of His Father on a continuous basis. The result? Giving and loving flowed out of Jesus' heart, mind, and mouth, like rivers of living water. His invitation to us is to drink deeply of Him, as He did of His Father, and whoever does so will be inundated with the receiving/giving dynamic of love (being loved and loving)—which then flows outward into laying down oneself so others might live.

In John 17, Jesus prayed that we would have the same oneness with the Father that He has. We receive this oneness through abiding in Jesus by the power of the Holy Spirit. Certainly it was the God-Man who won the cosmic war with Satan; however, Jesus *in His humanity* received the download of love from His Father (becoming the perfect human image of God's love), and now passes this image onto us as we drink of Him and abide in Him.

Jesus laid down His life that we might live. Truly this is a great love, mirroring the love of God who *gave* His Son that we could receive life and be restored to Him: "For God so loved the world that He gave His only begotten Son, that whoever believes in [into] Him should not perish but have everlasting life" (John 3:16).

And the "everlasting life" we receive is a life typified by the capacity to love everyone, even our enemies, as God does. I know that I need Jesus' capacity within me in order to fully and humbly love in this way. How about you?

Summary: Choosing Jesus

In fixing our eyes on Jesus, the character trait that comes into focus in a startlingly clear way is His total reliance upon His Father by continually *communing* with Him. Jesus made sure His human spirit was in communication with His Father, and with the Spirit who flowed between Them.

This was the Source-Water for Jesus to drink of and swim in daily. As conformed to Him, it is to be the primal Source-Water for *us* to swim in and drink of as well. I am still riddled with vestiges of doubts and self-solutions to life—self-reliance. Yet, I know that God-reliance is a fundamental reality to pursue on a daily basis as I seek to become the image of God that He created me to be.

Likewise, eating and drinking Jesus means that I continuously invite the Holy Spirit to make exchanges in my heart that I might progressively bear an image-imprint of Jesus' keen *moral discernment*. He walked boldly in truth through His 33 years on earth, unafraid to confront and expose evil whenever He encountered it.

Even in this moment, I ask the Holy Spirit to bring to my awareness places in my soul where moral sensitivity has been dulled by self-gratification; where I have been lulled to insensitivity by the apathetic ways of the world; and where I have been weakened by fear of consequences if I were to confront evil and provoke its wrath. I commit further to willingly allow the Lord to make the heart exchanges necessary to have Jesus' moral discernment reign within my soul.

Finally, and most of all, may the Holy Spirit continue to realign the misalignments of my thoughts, my emotions, my intentions, and my actions . . . that in all of these dimensions the Holy Spirit may accomplish heart exchanges that will expand soul-qualities of *giving* and loving.

I believe the deepest, most God-like hardwiring of human nature is the precious dynamic of love, towards God and towards all others. It bears repeating, "God is love" (1 John 4:16). **The core of God's heart is self-giving and, as made in His image, the core of my heart is also to be this same self-giving.**

There is a song whose words speak of God having put millions of doors in the world for His love to walk through, "and one of those doors is you." There is a poem that says I am a hole in a flute through which Christ's breath is to move, so that everyone I meet can hear His music.

I affirm truth in both of these metaphors but think it important to drill down into what it means for humans to be a "door" or a "flute," lest the *passive* action of a "let go, let God" channeling be signified by these images.

I am neither a door nor a flute. I am a complex, organic, living person. Becoming a living image of God happens by my *continuous choices* to allow the Holy Spirit to make actual and specific exchanges in my thinking, feeling, willing—in the entire character, conversation, and conduct of my life.

Upon my active willing and desiring such exchanges, the Holy Spirit transforms my soul, that is, He realigns and reforms my soul by conforming it to Jesus. *Then* I am engaged in the process of becoming: a mind through which Jesus Christ's thoughts find expression; a heart that is a love-expression of Jesus' emotions and dispositions; and a will through which Jesus acts morally and lovingly in the world. Then, in truth, I am becoming the life and likeness of Jesus—a distinct and unique personal expression of Jesus—and I am truly becoming myself at the same time.

Chapter 17

Jesus Living in and through Us

The Master Artist

Building on the theme of the previous chapter, "A Masterpiece Restored," there is a Scriptural verse that highlights this artistic reference: "For we are God's own handiwork, His workmanship, recreated in Christ Jesus, born anew" (Ephesians 2:10 AMP).[11] The Greek word Paul chose for "workmanship" was *poiema,* from which the word *poem* is derived. Paul had just said, "But God who is rich in mercy, because of His great love with which He loved us, even when we were dead in trespasses, made us alive together with Christ" (v.5).

So, when God works on us as the Master Potter (Isaiah 64:8), He takes the inert clay of our lives into His mighty hands and shapes us into a reflection of Himself. *Poiema* is used in Ephesians 2:10 to convey a sense of God as the Master Craftsman creating something special in His human works of art. *Poiema* in this text has been translated as "masterpiece." Yes, we are God's masterpieces.

Continuing with the theme of God as Master Creator, in the third chapter of Ephesians Paul further develops the inner dynamics of God's creative process:

> May Christ through your faith actually dwell, settle down, abide, make His permanent home in your hearts! May you be rooted deep in love and founded securely on love . . . . That you may really come to know practically through experience

---

[11] The purpose of using the Amplified Bible is to bring out the richness of the Hebrew and Greek languages. It goes beyond the traditional word-for-word concept of translation. The Amplified Bible gives other, clarifying meanings that may be concealed by the traditional translation method, while also giving the single English word equivalent for each key Hebrew and Greek word. For easier reading I have removed brackets and parentheses in the text.

for yourselves the love of Christ, which far surpasses mere knowledge without experience; that you may be filled through all your being, unto all the fullness of God; that you may have the richest measure of the divine Presence, and become a body wholly filled and flooded with God Himself!

(Ephesians 3:17-19 AMP)

It is clear from this passage that God's desire and intention is to indwell the innermost being and personality of humans. This is how He creates us anew, how He molds and shapes us into new creations (2 Corinthians 5:17). Romans 5:5 confirms this inflow of God's love: ". . . the love of God has been poured out in our hearts by the Holy Spirit who was given to us."

Not a Personal Growth Model

Although the powerful passage from Ephesians above can at first glance appear to be a promo for self-improvement and self-development, the opposite is true. God's masterpieces are not stand-alone works of art to be hung in a gallery. Coupling Ephesians 3:17-19 with John 7:37-38, we see that God's intention of filling us up with His love is so we can pour it out onto others. Becoming filled and flooded with the inwardly transforming love of Jesus has an outward, self-giving movement, ". . . out of his heart will flow rivers of living water" (v. 38). Rivers of loving others.

Jesus' life and teaching were *against* self-realization. The entire gesture of Jesus is *self-expenditure*. Yes, God wants to fill us up until we are beautiful, plump grapes, but in becoming like Jesus, this means squeezing the juice out to nourish others. As described throughout this book, the nature of sin is the nature of self-realization, in that the basic belief undergirding self-realization is: *I am my own god*. I believe that this entrenched self-deification is mainly what has sealed the doom of the old self, inherited from fallen Adam and Eve. The first principle in the Kingdom, above all, is that we worship nothing else in our lives but the one true God (Exodus 20:3).

So, although the focus of this book is personal transformation, I hope it is clear by now that I am not advocating a personal-growth model of self-improvement. Becoming like Jesus means that I allow the Holy Spirit to make me a new creation by redirecting and realigning my mind, heart, and will in ways that re-present (make present) Jesus' mind, heart, and will. It starts with immersing and abiding in Jesus, and becoming like Him as the Holy Spirit forms and conforms. And, as I have inwardly become more like Jesus, I can feel an unmistakable outward-moving energy towards loving, serving, and giving.

God is Love, and Jesus is humanity-infused Love. As I am formed into the likeness of Jesus (like a vase in the Master Potter's hands), I am becoming a person who more and more *desires* to serve others.

Let me express these thoughts with an illustration.

There is a story about a businessman who was a believer in Jesus. He and two of his associates were running through an airport to catch a plane. Delayed by unforeseen glitches in their business meeting in New York, the men were now hurrying to catch their flight back home to Chicago. As they turned a corner in the main terminal to head towards their gate, one of the men's briefcases hit a vendor's applecart. The jolt shook a large basket of apples on the cart and they began to tumble onto the floor of the terminal. One of the men glanced back over his shoulder as they kept running. He saw a young woman come out from behind the cart, scurrying around to pick up her apples. The men continued running down the concourse to their gate. It was Friday afternoon and they very much wanted to make the flight and return home to their families.

They made it to the gate just in time! With sighs of relief and joking banter, they walked down the aisle of the plane to their seats. Two of the men took their seats in a row of three seats, the third stood hesitantly by the aisle seat. "What's up, Jack?" said one of the men who noticed a concerned expression on Jack's face.

"I'm going back," said Jack. "I'll see you guys in Chicago when I can catch another flight." He turned and darted out of the plane, just before the flight attendant closed the hatch for takeoff. With startled expressions on their faces, the men watched Jack exit.

Upon returning to the scene of the accident, Jack saw the young woman on her hands and knees on the cement floor, feeling around for the scattered apples. She was blind. A few travelers had returned some apples that had rolled out into foot-traffic, but most folks were moving swiftly to catch their flights.

The businessman bent down and gently told the woman that he was helping her gather her apples and replace them in her basket. She was weeping but nodded her head in grateful assent.

When all was set right, the man apologized to the blind woman, and taking her small hand in his, he placed into it a $100 bill, telling her that he was doing so. He said that she should buy a new batch of apples because many of them were probably bruised by the fall.

The woman, who had stopped crying because of the man's kindness, now began weeping tears of joy and relief. With her hand still holding the money and the man's hand, she turned her face up towards his and asked, "Mister, are you Jesus?"

I don't know what the man replied since the story ends with her question, but my response is *yes, she had encountered Jesus*. I know that the man could have been a non-believer and acted the same way, and that humans of no particular religious affiliation can engage in such acts of kindness, but the businessman was a Jesus believer. I want to make some observations to highlight the theme of being conformed to the likeness of Jesus:

- The man could have had a relationship with God whereby there was a level of personal communing sufficient for him to hear the still, small voice within, prompting him to act, perhaps even prompting him to glance back over his shoulder while running down the concourse.
- The self-slant in the man could have rationalized that the girl would probably be alright if he didn't go back to help her, but a sharpened moral capacity in him might have been strong enough to discern the right thing to do—and *to do it* by choosing to ignore his self-slant (die to it) and let his *will* unite with the call of Love.

- He laid down his life for another. He loved his neighbor as himself, to the point of putting her above his self-interest.

These three observations mirror characteristics of how I believe humans are made in God's image, and how we are conformed to this image by being formed into the likeness of Jesus.

We all want to hear those words, "Well done, good and faithful servant" (Matthew 25:21). I believe that this response will come not because anyone has completed a checklist of good actions, but because he or she has stepped into the transforming process of becoming the likeness of Jesus.

Many religions have a balance-scale whereby entrance into heaven is seen as contingent upon one's good deeds outweighing the bad. The Gospel of Jesus Christ is different. He reveals a process of being born anew into a relationship with God in which we become new *beings* (2 Corinthians 5:17), not new *doings* (although new actions flow from new being).

It could have been the very nature and life of Jesus flowing out from that man in the airport, like a river of living water, and the blind girl sensed *His* presence, *His* character. It's not much of a stretch to think that Jesus was there, acting through one of His apprentices who was becoming the likeness of his Master.

Perhaps this story is a variant understanding of a prophecy from long ago: "And out of their gloom and darkness the eyes of the blind shall see" (Isaiah 29:18 NASB). The young woman was able to "see" Jesus because of the man who *presenced* Jesus through himself . . . the Incarnation of Jesus Christ continuing through a member of His Body here on earth (1 Corinthians 12:27).

Jesus laid down His life that we might live; now we can lay down our lives that He might live. Isn't this the way of living that will touch our Father's heart, prompting Him to say, "Well done good and faithful servants, my true sons and daughters"?

The Self: Dead or Alive?

In Matthew 16:24, Jesus says, "If anyone desires to come after Me, let him deny himself and take up his cross [instrument of execution] and follow me. For whoever desires to save his life will lose it, and whoever loses his life for My sake will find it." The understanding of this passage is found in Romans 6:11, "Likewise you also, reckon yourselves to be dead indeed to sin, but alive to God in Christ Jesus our Lord."

Paul understood what Jesus was saying because the Holy Spirit had led him into the radical transformation of considering his old self to be dead, replaced by being a new creation in Christ Jesus. After his encounter with Jesus on the road to Damascus, and three years wandering in the Arabian desert, his life was radically altered. Saul the persecutor of Jesus became Paul the ambassador of Jesus.

Throughout Paul's epistles, we find many references to the old nature we inherited from the first Adam, a nature that was replaced by the new nature in Jesus, "the last Adam" (1 Corinthians 15:45). We find words such as *the old man, the flesh, the old self*—all synonymous references to what we initially inherited.

What is the self? Is it not simply the individual, unified workings of a human mind, emotions, and will in a physical body? The self is a dynamic core in which each person's character and conduct are shaped in specific ways.

Similar to the chambers of the heart (both physical and spiritual) each individual self is a repository of whatever is poured into it. Then, like the heart, the contents are pumped out into the whole organism via thoughts, feelings, desires—all the way out into behavior.

When we speak of *self*, we may indeed be speaking of what Jesus said in Matthew 12:34-35: "For out of the abundance of the heart the mouth speaks. A good man out of the good treasure of his heart brings forth good things, and an evil man out of the evil treasure brings forth evil things." In Ezekiel 36:26, God says "I will give you a new heart," to replace the old heart of stone. I am not necessarily equating *self* with *heart,* but they are similar in meaning. [12]

I am a person named Bill Day, a unique human being, created in God's image. Over many years, the formation of my *self* that has taken place within my mind, emotions, and will has been severely and habitually bent inwardly towards my own egocentricity. This is a malformation that is beyond my capacity to unbend in the radical way that is warranted, in order to be an authentically loving, giving person. "Naturally," in my basic disposition, I am more self-centered than others-centered.

Galatians 2:20 says, "I have been crucified with Christ; it is no longer I who live, but Christ lives in me." It is the *old self* that we are to die to, in agreement with God's decision regarding the fate of our wrongly developed human nature. My old thinking, feeling and acting system (self) has died in Christ, but there is still a *me*—a particular *person* created to be a son in the family of God.

When the Holy Spirit comes into a person, the heart-exchange process of transformation is established (like toxin-removal and oxygenation in the physical heart). The Holy Spirit replaces wickedness and darkness with Jesus' capacity to love God instead of disrespecting Him . . . and to love one's neighbor instead of maligning him or her.

While we *remain* in Christ Jesus, the Holy Spirit creates everything anew—"a new creation" (2 Corinthians 5:17). The God-created *self-structure* (mind, emotions, will) is not innately bad, needing annihilation so we can live a supposedly self-less existence. We need to die to the *old* self, the false, self-absorbed "nature" that is irremediably riddled with missing the mark (sin) of what God intended. However, we need a self in order to love, to give, to serve— to live out our lives the way God intended. We need a *new* self.

---

[12] It is beyond the scope of this book to attempt a lengthy or definitive statement of either *self* or *heart*. This brief description is my attempt to express what I understand to be the *essence* of self. Both self and heart are words that have many definitions attached to them in theology, psychology, and the arts.

Jesus had a self. He speaks of "Myself" in John 5:30. In John 17:5, He refers to His Father's self when He prays, "And now, O Father, glorify Me together with Yourself." Jesus used His human mind, emotions and will to love and care for those around Him. When I am drawn into Him, I become a Jesus-and-Bill self. "Christ living in me" is a hybrid. **As I abide in Christ, the Holy Spirit recharges and re-aligns my spirit, and then re-aligns and reforms the mind, emotions, and will of the specific person that is *me*.**

The reason I bring up the subject of "self" is that in many sectors of Christendom, a focus on *dying to self* has overshadowed the other half of the equation in Romans 6:11: "being alive to God." The word *sanctification* means *to set aside*. Many Christians (myself included in years past) have made concerted efforts to set aside worldliness and to separate ourselves from vain things, as the way to die to the old self and to be holy.

But sanctification, in its positive sense, means *set aside unto God*: "Now if we died with Christ, we believe that we shall also live with Him" (Romans 6:8). We can see from this verse that the second half of the exchange, after dying, is *being filled with His enlivening Life*.

We release the *old self* and, in Jesus, receive a *new self* so we can live a fully robust, joyful life. Jesus said He came that we ". . . may have life . . . and have it more abundantly" (John 10:10). Focusing on cutting ourselves loose from the sinful ways of the world can cause critical and self-righteous character traits to develop. A self-denying mentality does not always produce a warm glow of love in our hearts. Sometimes it produces colorless Christians who are woeful witnesses of the vibrant, life-giving Person in whom they have placed their lives.

Let us fix our eyes on Jesus to understand the blueprint. Jesus was completely dead to sin and yet able to be *in* the world without being *of* the world. He didn't cut Himself off from the world, He immersed Himself in the world . . . a Light in a vast darkness. Through His constant communing with His Father, He was totally "alive to God." Wherever He went, love, light, and the joy of life radiated from Him in every direction.

Jesus poured out Himself (His self) in giving, caring, emptying out His life for others. He directed Himself inwardly towards communing with His Father, and outwardly towards serving, helping, encouraging, and laying down His life for others. This is the way of Jesus, and it is to be our way as well.

Far from annihilating our God-intended self, Jesus wants to re-create each self into the very image of Himself. It's Genesis 1:26 all over again: God breathing His Life into our nostrils anew, and we become *new* creations, though not new in the Mind of God. The person I am becoming, as I let my heart become one with the heart of Jesus, is the person I truly am in the Mind of God. Hence, as stated previously, the subtitle of this book: *and becoming yourself at the same time.*

Chapter 18

Ultimate Intention

Two Hearts Beating as One

Months ago, when looking through many icons, images, and paintings, in search of something for my book cover, I came upon a painting that riveted my attention. I contacted the artist and told him of my project, requesting permission to use his painting as my book cover. While talking with him, I learned that he had created the painting for his wife, giving it to her on their 25th wedding anniversary. Its title: *Two Hearts Beat As One.*

When the artist, Stephen, told me that he created his painting to celebrate 25 years of marriage, a poignancy struck me that I later explored during a time of communing with the Lord. In that prayer time, memories came to mind of being initially drawn into, and then willingly stepping into, the reality of Jesus Christ. It was as though I had been shocked to life by the Holy Spirit.

In the painting, you can see the life-pulse flowing between the two hearts. For me, this became the Love-impulse of Jesus giving my heart *His* life. This impulse is not an "electric shock" that awakens my old, deadened self. **Rather, I am shocked alive (regenerated) as a new creation, and given a new self in Christ Jesus, by the power of the Holy Spirit. "It is no longer I who live but Christ lives in me" (Galatians 2:20).**

I look at the painting (the book cover) and I see two hearts beating in unison because of the golden life-pulse that charges them both. I step into the painting and feel the Life of Jesus coursing through and charging my heart with His vitality. I know that this is the way I partake of the divine nature (2 Peter 1:4). I know that I am not alone, and that Jesus will never leave me nor forsake me (Hebrews 13:5). And I am reminded of Jesus' picture of abiding in Him as a branch in a vine (John 15:4). The Life-pulse of His heart charging and changing mine merges with an image of the sap enlivening a newly-grafted branch. In Him I am made whole and fully alive.

Scriptures came to mind during that quiet time I sought the Lord: "I will betroth you to Me forever; yes I will betroth you to Me in righteousness and justice, in lovingkindness and mercy; I will betroth you to Me in faithfulness, and you shall know the Lord" (Hosea 2:19-20). "For your Maker is your husband" (Isaiah 54:5).

Astonishing and unfathomable though it seems, I firmly believe we are called into a relationship with Jesus that is a likeness of the two-becoming-one intimacy of marriage (Genesis 2:24). I look again at the book cover and see the two hearts made synchronous by the golden life-pulse, and know that it is a *Love-pulse*. I see God's ineffable Love streaming out, Heart to heart, wooing me into a relationship wherein He pulls me to Himself in a love-embrace. There, in His embrace, He enlivens me, restores me, and makes me like Himself so I can be a suitable companion for all eternity.

Becoming the Likeness of Our Father

I look deeper into the painting and I see another heart, the heart of the Father. As Jesus said, "I and My Father are one" (John 10:30), and "He who has seen Me has seen the Father . . . . I am in the Father, and the Father [is] in Me" (John 14:10-11).

In becoming one with the heart of Jesus, we are joined with the heart of Father God as well. In His heart we are indeed *home*.

The image of two hearts beating as one is meant to depict a believer's heart joined to the heart of Jesus by the life-giving, pulsing power of the Holy Spirit. However, the entire Trinity is involved because the heart of Jesus beats as one with the heart of His Father. Jesus prays ". . . that they all may be one as You, Father, are in Me, and I in You; that they also may be one in Us . . . that the love with which You loved Me may be in them, and I in them" (John 17:21-26). A significant addition to what it means to be conformed to the likeness of Jesus is to allow the Holy Spirit to create in one's heart the very likeness of the Person Jesus identifies as Father.

For this dimension of Father in the Godhead, I have been meditating on the story of the return of the prodigal son, recorded in Luke 15:11-32.

Imagine the scene in the story of the prodigal son in which the son has become convicted of his waywardness and has returned to his father. [13] You can imagine the son, in a heartfelt gesture of repentance, kneeling before his father. The father immediately embraces him and receives the shame and tears that pour out from his son. We see *sorrow* etched into the father's countenance, as well as a stirring gesture of *forgiveness* and love-without-reserve in the father's embrace of his son. Jesus tells this story; it is the story of His Father, and our Father

First, the sorrow. Just as the father grieved the loss of his son for many years, so also I can imagine the deep sorrow our heavenly Father has felt over the immense waywardness of His children throughout the centuries. God's grief is the sorrowful price that He willingly pays—the price that comes with His gift of free choice, without which love cannot blossom and grow. The grief of Father God is embodied in Jesus who took the full brunt of human waywardness upon Himself: "He is despised and rejected by men, a Man of sorrows and acquainted with grief" (Isaiah 53:3).

In my work, I have sometimes seen patients form distorted beliefs that God wasn't present when bad things had happened to them; or if He was acknowledged as present, they pictured Him as an apathetic bystander. The first belief is: *God wasn't there and He doesn't care.* A second belief goes something like: *If He was there, why didn't He do something about it (trauma, abuse, etc.)?* This second accusation against God often merges with the first belief to form a conclusion: *He doesn't care, because if He cared He would have intervened and prevented the abuse.* Anger at God screams out from these beliefs.

For decades, I myself carried around twisted, anger-laden beliefs such as these. It has been a true blessing to witness patients in Divine

---

[13] For a beautiful visual of this scene, search the Internet for photos of the painting, *The Return of the Prodigal*, by the Dutch artist, Rembrandt van Rijn (1606-1669). An inspiring commentary is *The Return of the Prodigal Son*, by Henri Nouwen.

Exchange Inner Healing sessions experience God as *grieving with them* in the pain caused by their choices or by pain-inflicting choices of others. It has also been life-changing for me to experience the grieving heart of God in my own healing. I know that during these sessions we are experiencing the true heart of the Father.

<u>Next, the forgiveness</u>. In the prodigal son story, imagine the gesture of the father's embrace of his son. "But when he was still a great way off, his father saw him and had compassion, and ran and fell on his neck and kissed him." (Luke 15:20). We see his embrace conveying a striking portrayal of unreserved forgiveness and love upon his wayward son.

Standing to the side, the elder son tries to break up the love-fest with resentment over his father not holding his younger brother accountable for his many misdeeds. But the father says the same thing to his elder son as he said to his servants: "It was right that we should make merry and be glad, for your brother was dead and is alive again, and was lost and is found" (Luke 15:32).

He had already told his elder son, "All that I have is yours" (v.31). To both sons, the father pours out his very life. He gives himself away without reserve, a portrayal of complete self-emptying and self-giving. This is not just a picture of a remarkable father. It is a depiction of God as the Fountainhead of all love, forgiveness, and joy—a Fountain of Love Who has no boundaries or limits.

Jesus is telling us in this story that the essential core of God is Compassion, Forgiveness, Generosity, and Lovingkindness. To be created in God's image and likeness, then, perhaps means something like having God's *spiritual DNA*. **We are hardwired and intended to be like our heavenly Dad—to be compassionate, caring, forgiving, and generous**. God's image became flawed and malformed in His human creatures, but Jesus carries the God-intended formation. In Him our hardwiring is recreated and restored to God's original design. In this sense, Jesus is truly *the master paradigm* of what we are to become.

In Jesus it is possible to have these capacities of Father God restored because He and the Father are one, and *His prayer will be answered: "*. . . that they also may be one in Us" (John 17:21).

Through Jesus, our Father calls us home. Home is in His arms, where He welcomes us with joy, forgiveness, and generous reinstatement as rightful heirs within His family.

~

The Incarnation is traditionally described as the divine Son of God coming to earth. In this book, I have said that I believe the Incarnation *continues* as we are conformed to the holy and loving character of Jesus. "Christ in us" is Jesus Christ continuing to come to earth in and through us.

And Jesus said, "He who has seen Me has seen the Father (John 14:9), so I will go further now, to say that God's plan is for the Father Himself to dwell on earth: "And I heard a loud voice from heaven saying, 'Behold, the tabernacle of God is with men, and He will dwell with them, and they shall be His people, and God Himself will be with them and be their God'" (Revelation 21:3).

Within my soul I hear the Spirit of God calling out a plaintive plea from the heart of the Father, a Father who is "not willing that any should perish" (2 Peter 3:9). The plea is for all God's children, like lost sheep, to hear the voice of the true Shepherd, the Lord Jesus, and to come Home:

> Do not fear, for I have redeemed you; I have called you by name; you are Mine! . . . Bring My sons from afar and My daughters from the ends of the earth, everyone who is called by My name, and whom I have created for My glory, whom I have formed, even whom I have made (Isaiah 43:1, 6-7 NASB).

I am coming towards the end of telling this long story. Speaking for myself, I have received God's forgiveness, and I have received His words: "Therefore you are no longer a slave but a son, and if a son, then an heir of God through Christ" (Galatians 4:7). Now, as I approach the age of 75, I sense an inner beckoning for me to reflect God's image by being my Father's embracing and welcoming arms. It is a beckoning to be, in myself, a point in space and time where all fellow human beings whom I meet can experience a glimpse of their true Home.

A Third Facet of the Diamond

Finally, impactful for humanity though it is for Jesus to have become sin for us that we might receive His rightly-aligned life (2 Corinthians 5:21), there is a reality that transcends the human dimension. After all, this is *God's* story—He's writing it and we are characters in it. At the cross, we have seen two beautiful facets of the Atonement Diamond: *the facet of forgiveness* and *the facet of transformation*. But there is a third facet of this Diamond, reflecting its light from all eternity: *the facet of the Bridegroom and His bride.*

Being "in Christ" isn't just about being forgiven and transformed— though these are precious. More and more I see that the whole panorama of salvation is about an overarching plan of God that includes us but is by no means only about us. In the beginning of this chapter, I referenced Scriptures that speak of God as our Husband (Hosea 2:19-20) and (Isaiah 54:5). I return to this image of marriage to reveal further depths of God's plan.

In the most intimate language known to mankind, the imagery of Bridegroom and bride is used in Revelation 19:7-9 NASB to depict the ultimate reality of what it means to be in Christ: "Let us rejoice and be glad and give the glory to Him, for the marriage of the Lamb has come and His bride has made herself ready . . . . Blessed are those who are invited to the marriage supper of the Lamb." In this image of bride and groom, the relationship of the Father providing a bride for His Son is pre-eminent in the storyline.

At the cross, there is a divine conspiracy of Love whereby God the Father makes the way for His Son to have His bride, promised from all eternity. The Divine Exchange of 2 Corinthians 5:21 includes this dimension of the eternal love between the Father and the Son, delivered and administered by the Holy Spirit.

Reconciliation, forgiveness, and personal transformation are central parts of God's overarching plan, but the context of all these actions is that we are being prepared to be the bride of Christ Jesus.

Whether we are in ministries of healing, cleansing, mentoring, or other ways of becoming the likeness of Jesus, it's all about being made ready for the marriage supper of the Lamb.

"Eye has not seen, nor ear heard, nor have entered into the heart of man the things which God has prepared for those who love Him" (1 Corinthians 2:9). The pre-existing relationship of the eternal Father with the eternal Son is incomprehensible to my finite mind, though I believe that one day I will understand more of this mystery. For now, I am content just to feel an inexplicable sense of worth to have been drawn into this grand plan.

I feel awe and wonder in realizing that God has so perseveringly pursued us with His Love, desiring not only that none should perish (2 Peter 3:9), but also that we would become transformed in such a complete way as to be a fit and suitable bride for His Son. That's pretty astonishing when you think about it!

Chapter 19

Assisting the Master

This final chapter outlines a few ways to cooperate with the Holy Spirit in His mission to make Jesus Christ real in our lives. I have presented what I believe to be a Biblical perspective: that transformation is *God's doing* through and through, and we need only to learn how best to *receive* what God so graciously *gives*.

However, this disposition of receptivity to God's transforming actions in us is not a state of passivity. Indeed, it takes a clear and conscious choice to ignore the clamoring of the old self attempting to jump into any situation, blurting out, "I'll take it from here!"

Who's in Charge?

One of the names of the Holy Spirit is "Helper" (John 14:16). He is not a helper in the sense of being an assistant, servant, or errand boy. The Holy Spirit is a Person in the Godhead, one of the three "Faces" of God, in whom we can see the dynamic power of God accomplishing His purposes.

From the outset of creation, we see that the Spirit of God was "hovering," not acting (Genesis 1:2). Then God said, "Let there be light" (Genesis 1:3). As soon as the Father issued the executive order, the Holy Spirit made it happen ". . . and there was light" (v.3). He is the Helper in the sense that He is the Executive Administrator within the Godhead. From the beginning, we have a picture of the Holy Spirit's mission as that of implementing, sustaining, and completing what the Godhead has planned.

Spirit is often translated as *Wind* or *Breath*, so when God *breathed* life into humankind in the first creation (Genesis 2:7), the Holy Spirit was dynamically involved. And in the regeneration (new creation) of being "born of the Spirit" (John 3:6), God the Holy Spirit breathes new life into humankind. Like *the wind*, says Jesus (v. 8).

In John 14:16, when Jesus describes the Holy Spirit as "another Helper," the word "another" means "another of the same kind," not a different kind. Jesus had been the disciples' *Paraclete* (one who comes alongside as a companion or helper) for three years. He says that He will send a *Paraclete* who is the same essence as Himself—same attributes of deity, same love, same power. This Helper is the Spirit of Truth who will abide with all disciples forever (John 14:16-17), and will "take of what is Mine [Jesus'] and declare it to you" (John 16:14).

Paul's letters then reveal that this Spirit will do this work of *re-presenting* and replicating Jesus, as we learn to "walk in the Spirit" (Galatians 5:16). The Holy Spirit will do this work not as some impersonal force but as a Person, like Jesus, and He will live within humans. *Immanuel* is not only *God with us*, but also *God in us*.

Returning to the opening theme of this chapter, I think it important to realize that we are in relationship with a Person when we speak of the Holy Spirit.[14] And further, this Person is a Helper in the sense that He is bringing about in us and on this earth the intentions of the entire Godhead. As the *Divine Helper God*, He is in charge of shaping our formation into the likeness of Jesus.

I have taken time to make this point about the Holy Spirit because many pulpits and books broadcast the supposed identity of the Holy Spirit as a kind of high-class executive assistant. This thinking implies that believers are the executives, bosses, and drivers. But, as the pithy bumper sticker counter-responds: IF GOD IS YOUR CO-PILOT, SWITCH SEATS.

A first suggestion for assisting the Master: Resist the old-self inclination that would try to consider the Holy Spirit as *your* assistant and *your* helper, here to take care of items on *your* agenda, and to show you how to live your life while *you* stay in the driver's seat.

Being born anew and becoming a new creation means that I am agreeing to receive my identity as a son or daughter—a relationship

---

[14] In my opinion, using "Ghost" to translate "Spirit" in the original King James translation was an unfortunate rendition, giving rise to impersonal, mystical, misty images of the third Person of the Trinity.

in which I am to die to a solo sense of myself, forever. Becoming a Jesus-in-me hybrid sets in motion a life that is to become more and more governed by the Holy Spirit. As John the Baptist proclaimed of Jesus, "He must increase, but I must decrease" (John 3:30).

Here again is the *exchange* principle that permeates the Gospel: Jesus takes unto Himself our old life and disposes of it, replacing it with His life. And the Holy Spirit is the executor and administrator of this transaction.

The Biblical presentation now seems clear to me: that when the Holy Spirit comes into a believer's life He comes in as *Master*. Transformation is a huge enterprise, way too much for human capabilities. The Holy Spirit is the Master Craftsman, the Potter, and we are to be clay in His hands.

What "doing" role does the clay have other than to remain in the Potter's capable hands, trusting Him to shape us into vessels of His design? Striving and trying with our old selves is like clay squirming and wriggling around, in futile attempts to "help" the Potter.

My old self jumps into many situations trying to re-establish its former dominance, but the Holy Spirit is teaching me and enabling me to ignore the old nature's clamoring for re-entry and dominance. **Refraining from acting on these impulses is a significant way of dying to the old self in me.** I'm a slow learner but I am getting better at recognizing when this self is making an appearance. *Tell-tale clues*: straining, worrying, controlling, manipulating, trying to steer and make things happen, and getting angry when things don't go my way.

I am now more aware that when I am in charge of something, like driving my car, I am in a particularly vulnerable position. My old self was accustomed to being in "the driver's seat" in my life and is always eager to jump in and take over. When I am driving a car, all it takes is for someone to cut in front of me and my old self can rear its ugly head in a moment, angrily grabbing at the reins to take control. It has not been easy but I now know that it is possible to be a co-pilot, even when sitting in the driver's seat of a car!

I don't always succeed in dying to (abstaining from, ignoring, releasing) this former self, but I have found a helpful *re-framing* suggestion that I want to share with you. Each day there are many opportunities in which I can choose to have the old self and its ways rule my life, or I can choose my new self in Jesus to hold sway. Since I believe that my "old man" was crucified with Jesus, and that I am "alive to God in Christ Jesus" (Romans 6:6, 11), whenever I let my old self have a presence and a voice in my life, I am pumping "life" into something I consider to be dead. In common parlance, we call this kind of entity a zombie.

These days there are many films about zombies—depictions of dead people being brought back to "life" by chemical or other means. The image of a zombie has become a graphic reminder to me that when, for example, I yell at a slow motorist in the passing lane, I am pumping consciousness and energy into my old self, enabling it to make its ghoulish appearance in my body and soul. <u>A second suggestion for assisting the Master</u>: Refuse to be a zombie.

I recently read about a strategy for dealing with cancer. It is called "intermittent fasting" and has been developed by observing that healthy cells are more adept than malignant cells in weathering the stressful effects of abstaining from food, for even short periods (16 hours). Healthy cells can more easily wait out the "lean period" of fasting, but cancer cells are more fragile and are weakened by fasting. Perhaps that is an encouragement for starving the old self so that our life in Christ can grow. Jesus-in-me is way stronger than my malignant old self.

Identity is Everything

In Chapter 5, I recounted the story of an event during which I experientially knew that I was "a son . . . an heir of God through Christ" (Galatians 4:7). I said that *it felt like the first day of my life* because finally I had a sense of belonging. I no longer felt alone but palpably experienced being in relationship with God as a beloved son.

Since that time, a special niche of my counseling practice has been ministering to men because of my strong conviction that God wants men to have this same experience. He wants the same for women— to know that they are beloved, precious daughters—but men are particularly prone to feel isolated and alone. A man can easily feel like an island.

A third suggestion for assisting the Holy Spirit is a plea to everyone to seek out help if you have any blocks in your soul that keep you from the experience of *knowing* you are beloved sons and daughters. Such an experiential awareness is a foundational piece of your identity, without which it is difficult to be receptive to the ongoing transformative work of the Holy Spirit. I impeded the transforming process for years by believing the lie that *I had gone too far and sinned too much to receive full forgiveness and be accepted as God's son.*

As the father of lies, Satan inserts false interpretations into many events of our lives—from early childhood into adulthood. These lies have to be flushed out into the open so they can be exposed and dispelled. When garbage piles (lies) are removed, rats (demons) flee.

I have received at least a dozen inner healing sessions facilitated by trained ministers and therapists. Numerous other Divine Exchanges have taken place directly between myself and the Lord. These healings have occurred during times when my heart has been troubled and I have prayerfully sought the Lord's truth about what was troubling me.

I encourage you to ask the Holy Spirit to expose the root of obstructions that may be lodged in your soul, keeping you from fully receiving the Lord's transforming ministry. If you have believed into the Lord Jesus, "you are no longer a slave but a son [daughter] . . . then an heir of God through Christ" (Galatians 4:7). Don't settle for less. Receive the fullness of who you are in Christ Jesus. The Holy Spirit wants to make *you* just like Jesus. His likeness is who you really are.

Communing with God

While preparing to write this segment on interacting with God, magnets and magnetism kept coming to my attention. I have in mind a large iron bar that has been permanently magnetized, upon which a smaller, unmagnetized iron bar is placed. As the small bar remains on the magnet, slowly but surely its electrons line up in the same direction as those of the large magnet. The smaller bar thereby also becomes a magnet. It becomes a *likeness* of the magnet upon which it rests. In our relationship with Jesus, we become personally aligned with Him, magnetized by Him into His likeness.

The following are some ways that I have found helpful in assisting the Master Craftsman to accomplish His artistry of bringing believers into this personal alignment, affording Him the opportunity of creating the masterpieces He intends:

Meditation and obedience: they go together. Reading and meditating on God's Word is an essential part of my daily time with the Lord, allowing me to soak into and attach to God as He "magnetizes" me to Himself. However, because the *personal* dimension is involved here, becoming the likeness of Jesus goes beyond inorganic magnetizing. The personal dimension brings *choice* into play.

I have previously commented on the belief coming out of the Contemplative Movement, purporting that meditation is an end in itself, that soaking in God's presence produces soul changes by a kind of spiritual osmosis. But, again, the gift of human free choice is essential. We become like Jesus when we allow (choose) the Holy Spirit to form the new life of Jesus in us as He replaces the old life we are willing to release (die to).

One of the most undervalued qualities of Jesus is His life of obedience. He aligned His will with His Father's will because He trusted and loved His Father. Out of love He said, "I always do those things which please Him" (John 8:29). And towards the end of His earthly sojourn, He said, "I have kept My Father's commandments, and abide in His love" (John 15:10). For Jesus, obedience was a way to abide in and bond with Father God.

For us, obedience is often a difficult word because we have been subjected to human abuses of power—coercive and intimidating commands, given to assert power rather than to promote wellbeing and love. Sometimes obedience has meant a blind adherence to rules out of fearful compliance with a rigid "because I said so" authority figure.

Jesus invites us into *His* kind of obedience, and He clearly presents it as a significant relationship-gateway to the fulfillment God intends for us. In John 14:21 Jesus says, "He who has My commandments and keeps them, it is he who loves Me." And He adds (verse 23), "If anyone loves Me, he will keep my word; and My Father will love him, and We will come to him and make Our home with him."

I don't always find obedience easy, but slowly I am allowing the Holy Spirit to conform me to Jesus' likeness in this personality trait too. Often it is an action of faith and trust, choosing to let my will be magnetized and aligned with God's will, even when I don't yet see a good result from doing so. However, I have taken on enough of Jesus' ways to know that God's commands are not tests to make me come to heel, like a dog. His commandments are *promises of blessing*. He really does know what is best for me, what will be most fulfilling in the long term.

As I have allowed the Holy Spirit to make me less self-absorbed and more a man of integrity, compassion, and generosity, I have experienced a huge increase in joy, peace, and wholeness as I become more myself than ever before. And it is truly awesome for such a former lawless rebel as myself to experience this fullness as a result of obedience!

<u>Spiritual Disciplines: they're about relationship</u>. The classic list of "spiritual disciplines" usually includes solitude, silence, study, prayer, service to others, and fasting. Historically, these disciplines have often been practiced to accomplish or earn something. Like the word obedience, *discipline* has taken on negative connotations of restraint, legalism, and restriction.

A study of the Gospels reveals that Jesus engaged in all of these disciplines, not as ends in themselves but as means to know, love, and trust His Father. For Jesus, doing these disciplines moved Him in the direction of the most important commandment: "You shall love the Lord your God with all your heart, and with all your soul, and with all your mind, and with all your strength" (Deuteronomy 6:5; Mark 12:30). He understood that spiritual disciplines are ways of getting into the right frame of mind and heart in order to hear and know God.

Our churches are filled with folks who consider their profession of faith in Jesus as a completed action. Done. Finished. They say, "I believe" and then move on to pursue other goals in their lives. You may or may not agree with me, but after reading this book, my hope is that you will consider that a profession of faith in Jesus is much more the "I do" of a marriage ceremony than an "I believe" mental assent. God woos us into a life-long relationship with Him in which all the elements of intimate relationship pertain.

What does it take for a marriage relationship to flourish? For sure, making it a *top* priority—lots of time, energy, listening, sharing, sacrifice, friendship, and committed love. There is an old joke about a wife approaching her husband as he sits in his recliner reading the newspaper. She says wistfully, "You never tell me anymore that you love me." He puts down his newspaper long enough to make emotionless eye contact and says, "I told you ten years ago when we married that I love you; if I change my mind I'll let you know." With that he returns to his newspaper. We may chuckle at that joke but there is pain as well as humor in that chuckle.

I believe that laziness, pride, and lack of relationship-focus have become built into human lives as a result of the Fall. Doing things "my way," and "for my benefit," often means oodles of time and energy for projects related to my self-interest. However, the two-way mutuality of relationships (with God and with others) warrants investments of time, energy, self-sacrifice, and passionate involvement. I believe that the Holy Spirit has the desire and the power to make *relationship* a higher priority than *self* in our lives, but we have to be willing for Him to do so.

The choice to ask the Holy Spirit to reveal and deal with this inborn laziness and lack of making relationship with Him a top priority is an important choice in assisting the Master to do His work of restoring the image of God in us. There is resistance from our old nature to engage in such practices as solitude, prayer, and fasting because they are practices that enhance the development of a relationship with God. *The old self is not interested in a relationship with God; it believes only in self-reliance.*

Choosing these practices and being willing to make relationship-building a top priority in our lives are significant ways of cooperating with the Holy Spirit. I believe He is always beckoning us into deeper levels of intimacy with God, and with one another.

Interacting with the Word of God. The *written Word* is a powerful touchstone for the *living Word*, who is Jesus (John 1:1). When I read Scripture, I pray at the same time for the Holy Spirit to speak the reality of God's presence through the medium of words—that the Living Word would come alive in me by the written Word. The intention is to have a person-to-person encounter. For this, the disciplines of solitude, silence, study, and sometimes fasting are helpful.

The analogy of the bar of iron resting on the magnet comes to mind again. I want to soak into the Word in such a way that "Deep calls to deep" (Psalm 42:7), that I open to and yield to what I experience coming through God's Word. I want to take the time for the magnetizing effect of His Love and Truth to permeate and realign my heart and mind as the Holy Spirit continues His conforming work.

Let me share a specific way I interact with Scripture. Sometimes I begin my day by lying on the floor on my back, my arms outstretched such that my body is in the form of a cross. I recite aloud Galatians 2:20: "I have been crucified with Christ; it is no longer I who live, but Christ lives in me; and the life which I now live in the flesh I live by faith in the Son of God, who loved me and gave Himself for me."

I say the words slowly, aware that I am in the presence of the Living Word. I ask the Holy Spirit to reveal anything in me that belongs to my old self (some sort of self-slant) and is "ripe" and ready to be released (acknowledged to have been crucified). If anything comes to mind, I ask the Holy Spirit to actualize His Divine Exchange (2 Corinthians 5:21) as I confess or release whatever comes to mind, and then receive in its place some aspect of Jesus' risen nature. I also ask that, during the day, He will keep me mindful of times when the old self may rear its head looking for a chance to assert itself.

Another way I interact with the Word is to say Psalm 139:23-24 as a person-to-person prayer. I *speak* to God by saying, "Search me, O God, and know my heart; try me, and know my anxieties; and see if there is any wicked way in me, and lead me in the way everlasting." Then I shift gears and listen to what He might want to show me or tell me.

Members of His Body

The concept and reality of *community* has been gradually weakening in the world through a relentless quest for self-determination. People are busier (and lonelier) than ever. Time-saving technology has promoted this hyperactivity, and we then tend to pull into ourselves to cope—thus accenting the overemphasis on individualism. However, God's hardwiring of us remains true: that we are created as individuals, but as individuals who are to exist in relationship with Him and with one another.

"For as the body is one and has many members, but all the members of that one body, being many, are one body, so also is Christ" (1 Corinthians 12:12). This book would not be complete without mentioning this corporate sense of Jesus' presence on earth. <u>Living in community provides a significant *context* for our transformation</u>. My wife and I belong to a local fellowship of Jesus believers, and we cherish the fact that it is both a place to receive soul nourishment and a place in which we can let flow out to others what God has deposited in us. It is important to us that this Fellowship of Christ is not an isolated colony of hermits. Rather, in our fellowship we help one another grow in spiritual maturity and in human maturity, and we encourage one another to love all others well—whomever and wherever we may encounter them. Through us, equipped in this way, Jesus reaches out to a darkened, deadened world.

Chapter 6 of Luke's Gospel provides a comprehensive vignette of how Jesus lived out His human hardwiring. In verse 12, we see Jesus finding the solitude of a mountain to commune with His Father during the night and early morning hours. Then He formed community around Himself by gathering together His apostles and disciples (v. 13-16). As a group, they went out with Him to minister to the poor, to preach the Kingdom of God, and to care for all who were afflicted. In

Jesus we see a wonderful balance of the personal and the corporate, a balance of His relationship with God and with others.

Coming Home

In John 8:12 NASB, Jesus said, "I am the Light of the world; he who follows Me will not walk in the darkness, but will have the Light of life." Jesus let the vast darkness that had overwhelmed all of creation fall upon Him. He absorbed that darkness so He could dispose of it and replace it with Himself as the Light of life. *He is still the Light of life.*

We have been invited into this amazing cosmic drama by Jesus Himself: "While you have the Light, believe in [into] the Light, so that you may become sons [and daughters] of Light" (John 12:36 NASB). *He is still inviting us into the Light.*

Jesus said, "I am the Way, I am the Truth, and I am the Life" (John 14:6 The Passion Translation). *He is still speaking these words to us.*

As we release our old darkened lives to Jesus and receive the Holy Spirit's work of transforming us into God's masterpieces, we are gradually becoming beacons of Light, beckoning all to see the Light and to know that there is a Way to come Home, where we belong.

In this the love of God was manifested toward us,

that God has sent His only begotten Son into the world,

that we might live through Him.

~ 1 John 4:9 ~

For He made Him who knew no sin

to be sin for us,

that we might become the righteousness of God in Him.

~ 2 Corinthians 5:21~

Postscript

This is the story I was led to tell. It is one traveler's story among many. If you would like to share your story or dialogue with me, I can be contacted at **billday@healingtroubledhearts.com**. If there is sufficient interest, I may start a blog so readers can share their transformation stories with one another. If a blog develops, I will post a notice on my website: **www.healingtroubledhearts.com.**

Thank you for giving of your time to read this story. May God who calls Himself Lovingkindness bless you mightily as you continue seeking truth.

Selected and Recommended Bibliography

Beilby, James (ed.). *The Nature of the Atonement*. Downers Grove, IL: IVP Academic, 2006.

Bromiley, G.W. (ed.) *The International Standard Bible Encyclopedia*. Grand Rapids, MI: Wm. B. Eerdmans Publishing, 1979.

Chambers, Oswald. *My Utmost for His Highest*. Grand Rapids, MI: Discovery House, 1992.

Dalbey, Gordon. *Healing the Masculine Soul*. Dallas: Word Publishing, 1988.

Day, William. *Healing Troubled Hearts*. Buffalo, MN: Pyramid Publishers, 2014.

Eldredge, John, and Brent Curtis. *The Sacred Romance*. Nashville, TN: Thomas Nelson, 1997.

Fromke, DeVern. *Ultimate Intention*. Indianapolis, IN: Sure Foundation, 1963.

Guyon, Jeanne. *Experiencing the Depths of Jesus Christ*. Sargent, GA: Christian Books Publishing House, 1975.

Hoff, BJ. *The Penny Whistle*. Minneapolis, MN: Bethany House, 1996.

Huegel, F.J. *Bone of His Bone*. Fort Washington, PA: CLC Publications, 2009.

Jabay, Earl. *The Kingdom of Self*. Plainfield, NJ: Logos International, 1974.

Jones, Peter. *One or Two: Seeing a World of Difference*. Escondido, CA: Main Entry Editions, 2010.

Keller, Timothy. *King's Cross*. New York: Penguin Group, 2011.

Kraft, Charles H. *Deep Wounds, Deep Healing*. Ventura, CA: Regal Books, 1993.

Kurath, Edward. *I Will Give You Rest*. Post Falls, ID: Divinely Designed, 2003.

Kylstra, Chester and Betsy. *Restoring the Foundations*. Santa Rosa Beach, FL: Proclaiming His Word, 2001.

Lehman, Karl. *The Immanuel Approach*. Evanston, IL: Immanuel Publishing, 2016.

Lewis, C.S. *Mere Christianity*. Riverside, NJ: Macmillan Publishing, 1952.

Lyons, Eric and Thompson, Bert. *In the "Image and Likeness of God."* Montgomery, AL: Apologetics Press, 2002.

McGrath, Johanna and Alister. *Self-Esteem: the Cross and Christian Confidence*. Wheaton, IL: Crossway Books, 2002.

Murray, Andrew. *Abide in Christ*. New Kensington, PA: Whitaker House, 1979.

Murray, Andrew. *The True Vine*. Chicago: Moody Publishers, 2007.

Murray, John. *Redemption Accomplished and Applied*. Grand Rapids, MI: Eerdmans Publishing, 1955.

Nee, Watchman. *The Spiritual Man*. New York: Christian Fellowship publishers, 1977.

Nouwen, Henri. *The Return of the Prodigal Son*. New York: Doubleday, 1992.

Paxson, Ruth. *Life on the Highest Plane*. Chicago: Moody Press, 1942.

Payne, Leanne. *Restoring the Christian Soul*. Grand Rapids, MI: Baker Books, 1991.

Penn-Lewis, Jessie. *Life in the Spirit*. Fort Washington, PA: CLC Publications, 1991.

Pink, Arthur. *An Exposition of Hebrews*. Grand Rapids, MI: Baker Book House, 1954.

Prince, Derek. *The Divine Exchange*. Charlotte, NC: Derek Prince Ministries, 1995.

Seamands, David A. *Healing Your Heart of Painful Emotions*. New York: Inspirational Press, 1993.

Smith, Edward M. *Theophostic Basic Training Seminar Manual*. Campbellsville, KY: New Creation, 2007.

Smith, Warren. *The Light that Was Dark*. Magalia, CA: Mountain Stream Press, 2005.

Takle, David. *The Truth About Lies And Lies About Truth*. Pasadena, CA: Shepherd's House, 2008.

Tapscott, Betty. *Inner Healing Through Healing of Memories*. Kingwood, TX: Hunter Publishing, 1975.

Thompson, Curt. *Anatomy of the Soul*. Carol Stream, IL: Tyndale House, 2010.

Virkler, Mark and Patti. *4 Keys to Hearing God's Voice*. Shippensburg, PA: Destiny Image Publishers, 2010.

Willard, Dallas. *Hearing God*. Downers Grove, IL: Intervarsity Press, 1999.

Also by the Author

In a previous book, *Healing Troubled Hearts*, Bill Day opens a window through which to see Christian inner healing and its Scriptural basis. This prior work also gives guidelines and steps for the ministry of Divine Exchange Inner Healing. *Healing Troubled Hearts* and *Becoming the Likeness of Jesus* are available from Amazon or from <u>healingtroubledhearts.com</u>

"In *Healing Troubled Hearts*, Bill Day has made an invaluable contribution to the literature regarding how we can engage with God in order to heal our brokenness. Bill's multi-faceted background and painstaking journey uniquely qualify him to speak with wisdom to address many of the mis-understandings about inner healing that are so prevalent today. I heartily recommend this work to anyone who still has questions about whether or not Christians need inner healing, and whether or not this ministry is a work of God."

David Takle, M.Div., author of *The Truth About Lies And Lies About Truth*

CPSIA information can be obtained
at www.ICGtesting.com
Printed in the USA
FFOW04n1855140218
45101709-45523FF